World Beyond World
God, Mankind and the Truth

CHAM Publishing Company

World Beyond World
by Woo Myung

First published in Korean September 2003
Fifth printing December 2003
Second edition July 2004
English edition May 2005

Published by CHAM Publishing Company, President Chang Hee Choi
Hapjeongdong 360-1, Mapoku, Seoul 121-884, Korea
Phone 82-2-325-4192/4
Facsimile 82-2-325-1569
E-mail chambooks@maum.org
Korean Registration No.13-1147, Date 2000. 12. 29

ISBN 89-87523-19-5 03100

This book has been translated into English
from the original 'World Beyond World' written in Korean in 2003.
Translated by Seung Min Lee, Mi Young Jung, Margie Conboy,
and Myung Hyun Hong.
For more information about Maum Meditation, go to http://www.maum.org

World Beyond World

God, Mankind and the Truth

Woo Myung

ABOUT THE AUTHOR

Woo Myung was born in a small town called Eui-sung which is located in the Kyungbook province of South Korea. The many struggles he experienced throughout life provided him with a yearning for peace, which, through introspection, opened his mind to the search for Truth. While operating an educational publishing house, he focused much of his energy on meditation, and eventually achieved enlightenment. In January of 1996, while meditating in the Gaya Mountains of South Korea, he became the Truth. That same year, he founded Maum Meditation and has been working ever since to educate the public on the maum (Korean for 'mind') and the Truth.

For his efforts he was awarded the Mahatma Gandhi Peace Award by the United Nations International Association of Educators for World Peace (IAEWP) in September of 2002. Woo Myung has also been appointed as a United Nations World Peace Ambassador.

He is the author of numerous books on discovering the Truth including Wisdom for Life (1996), The Natural Flow of the Universe (1998), True Mind (1998), The Enlightened World (1998), World Beyond World (2003), Forever Living world (2004), and The Formula from Heaven that will Save the World(2005). His 7th book, 'The Formula from Heaven that will Save the World' (2005), includes many of his artistic drawings and poems of which there is an anthology of over 1 million works including songs written and recorded by Woo Myung.

Cover illustration-
The cover illustration was drawn by Woo Myung. It is a graphical summation of the Maum Meditation method, and is titled "The Formula from Heaven that will Save the World."(1) The Universe minus (2) Human Mind and Body minus (3) The Stars, the Sun, the Moon and the Earth equals (4) The Emptiness equals (5) The Heaven, World Beyond World

World Beyond World

Because I don't exist, the True I exists
Because this world doesn't exist
The True world exists
World beyond world
It is the world that exists when I don't exist
When this world doesn't exist
It is the True world that can be obtained
When my mind is the highest, the widest, the biggest
The world of God
The world of oneness
The world of forever everlasting
The world of no burden, no suffering
The world of freedom, liberation
Where everybody lives as one

CONTENTS

CHAPTER 3. THE KINGDOM OF LIGHT

POSTSCRIPT

APPENDIX - DIALOGUES ON GOD, EXISTENCE AND THE TRUTH

● FOREWORD

In the year 2002, I had an opportunity to talk about world peace with the Chairman of the General Assembly at the United Nations Headquarters. At that time, I proposed the most essential solution in peacefully bringing all of the world's conflicts to an end. The proposal is for all people around the world to become one, to become the Truth, regardless of nationality, ethnic background, and religion, through the process of cleansing the mind.

People have different ways of thinking, and each individual lives life according to his own viewpoint, always thinking that his way is right.

When I was young, I often thought that I could never live happily while those around me were suffering from poverty, and there would be no point of living a life of fortune for only myself. However, I stifled those thoughts for a period of time as I, myself, struggled with difficulties in life. I pondered about whether there was a way to be set free from pain and the heavy burdens set upon me. Thus I became interested in many religious books.

I believed God or Buddha existed within me. I knew my mind must be cleansed in order to find my true self, which eventually led me to know the Truth. After becoming the Truth, I left my worldly life and founded Maum Meditation and have been teaching people this practice ever since.

I realized in this period of time of the universe, my destiny is to let the entire world know of the path to becoming God, which, until now, has been an unattainable quest for mankind. This book contains the lectures I have given in America to many religious leaders, theologians, and philosophers to answer their questions and inquiries about the Truth.

July 2003 Washington D.C.

Woo Myung

CHAPTER 1
MIND IS THE WHOLE OF THE UNIVERSE

How to Become the Truth

Since childhood, I have been searching for answers to questions: Where does man come from? Why is man here? Where does man go after death? But there was no way to find answers to these questions.

After my father passed away when I was nine years old, I became fearful of life and death and felt very lonely. Since then, I had been thinking a lot about those questions, but I was not able to find the answers. In my thirties I began searching for answers to these questions through religious studies and spiritual readings. Still, I did not find the answers.

In order to find answers on my own, I planned to examine life's questions through meditation by going into the mountains where I would be surrounded by nature. I decided to follow my plan after I secured a livelihood earning money in the academic profession. Then I would leave the routine life.

At the end of 1995 through the beginning of 1996, I spent time at Gaya Mountain in Korea to eliminate my past life experiences through a meditation process. At that time my wife had not been interested in the pursuit of discovering the Truth. Eventually, however, she understood my deep conviction and desperation, and wanted to come to Gaya Mountain and meditate with me. Initially, I did not want her to join me because I myself had not found the answers even though I had been meditating for a few months. I thought that if she came with me I would not be able to focus solely on my meditation. My wife continued to insist on coming with me, but I continued to refuse. I kept pondering over whether or not she should come. Finally, I decided that since I was meditating on how to become a saint then it would also be good for my wife to study to become a saint.

We then went to Gaya Mountain together and my wife became enlightened after only three days and two nights of meditation. At that time I had already spent three months, but I still had not attained enlightenment. When my wife became enlightened, I heard her rejoicing from the next room. She did not outwardly reveal her enlightenment directly to me because she was concerned that, if she told me of her enlightenment, I would be distracted from my meditation. I was happy that my wife became enlightened as I felt better for at least one of us to be enlightened rather than neither of us.

I continued to recall my past life experiences and realized that I was the greatest sinner of all. Since I was such a sinner, I did not think it would be possible to become a saint. I thought that if I became a saint the world would laugh at me. After realizing that everything was my fault, I decided I must completely kill myself in my mind. I did not sleep for a few nights and kept killing mercilessly.

Finally, the Truth was revealed and I realized that the Truth is I, myself. At that moment, I met Jesus, Buddha and many other saints in heaven. Also I realized that because I am the Truth, my destiny is to teach the Truth to all mankind. Since November of 1996 I have been teaching the Truth to others. In June 1997, I ended my academic career and focused solely on teaching the Truth to others.

In the beginning I gave one instruction per month. As more became involved, I instructed twice per month and gradually increased the frequency of my instruction to four times per month. Now, over two hundred thousand people have been involved in Maum Meditation, and many of them have become the Truth.

How Can One Reach the Truth and Why Must We Become the Truth?

First, we must know what the Truth is.
What is the Truth?

We have learned that the Truth is never changing and everlasting. Then, what exactly is the never changing and everlasting existence? Let's begin by thinking about the universe. The universe cannot be drawn because it is infinite, however, let's try representing it this way:

The infinite universe contains the stars, the sun, the moon, and the earth, and on this earth, man lives. Just as what we see and what we hear is the Truth, what we see here is the whole of the universe.

There are the stars, the sun, the moon, and the earth in the universe.

Now, let's think back when man lived on this earth with

the sun, the stars, and the moon a long, long, long time ago. Imagine living at that time a long, long, long time ago, trillions of trillions years ago. Scientists say the life span of stars ranges from 5 to 14 billion years. Thus, during that time, the stars, the sun, the moon, the earth, and man would have all disappeared. Compared to the trillions of trillions years, the 14 billion years of the life span of stars is like a split second. Thus, everything is gone and only pure emptiness remains.

Now, imagine the hottest fire burning all of that emptiness from trillions years ago until now. Does the emptiness disappear? No, it remains. It is the never changing and everlasting existence.

The emptiness, which is the universe before the infinite universe, is the Truth. This emptiness has existed forever without beginning and end, and lives forever and ever.

Just as we all have body and mind, this infinite universe also has body and mind. The body is the emptiness. The mind, which is the one God, omnipresent in the entire universe, fills the entire emptiness.

The reason why man cannot see the God of the universe is because of man's self-centered attachments. Because man is confined to his own shape, man can never see the Great

Soul and Spirit that is the mind and body of the universe.

Thus, man cannot know or become the universe. Only when man becomes the Great Soul and Spirit will man be able to see and know the Great Soul and Spirit. Because of man's self centered attachments, which is sin, man cannot become one with the Truth.

The Great Soul and Spirit is the creator. This Great Soul and Spirit creates the stars, the sun, the moon, the earth, all creation, and mankind.

We learned in science class that the stars, the sun, the moon, the earth, all creation, and mankind came from the universe. This is the Soul and Spirit of the Truth. Man can never live eternally unless he returns to this existence of the Truth, which is the Soul and Spirit.

The method to become this Great Soul and Spirit is to throw away the self centered human mind and the body that contains it. We then must throw away our delusional universe as well. Only then the Great Soul and Spirit remains.

When one's mind and body is reborn as the Great Soul and Spirit itself, he is reborn as the child of God. This is resurrection. This is eternal, everlasting life. This Great Soul and Spirit itself is I, myself. I am the Truth itself.

 When one is reborn as this Great Soul and Spirit itself, he lives forever as the eternal God because the whole is the individual and the individual is the whole. He becomes the energy and light of the universe itself, which is the everlasting Truth.

The individual who becomes the Great Soul and Spirit of the universe, which is the Truth, has heaven. A person whose mind becomes as big as the Great Soul and Spirit of the infinite universe can live forever in  heaven. To become the Great Soul and Spirit itself, one must throw away his mind, body, and even the universe through the Maum Meditation method. Then, he becomes the Great Soul and Spirit itself and lives forever as everlasting, eternal God. This is human completion. The Bible, the Buddhist Sutras, and the scriptures of other religions are all about this.

Now that we know what the Truth is, I will explain heaven and hell.

The difference between heaven and hell is that heaven is the world where the Great Soul and Spirit of the universe live, and hell is where one lives knowing only what he has experienced from the past and where life is limited to that of the shadow of memories.

Last night I dreamt I was in a battlefield. Gunfire was coming from all directions and all our troops were killed. I knew I must run to the mountain 50 miles away to escape the enemy. Having been shot in the left leg, I struggled to run. Not realizing I was in a dream, the sufferings I was feeling seemed real. All night long, I dreamt of running in the battlefield under a shower of never-ending gunfire. Just as I had reached the mountain, the enemy opened fire upon me. At that moment I woke up and realized that I was not in the battlefield, there was no gunfire, and I had not been shot. The dream was an illusion.

Although dreams exist, they are not reality but illusions. Dreams exist, but at the same time they do not exist because they are illusions, false reality. Like the dream that appears to be real, man lives as the shadow of his memories which is the experience of his past life, his self-centered attached mind. The life of man is a dream.

Man lives in a dream-like mind. Suppose one has lived with this mind until the age of 40. He will continue to live with the same mind until he is 90, and he will live with that same mind even after death.

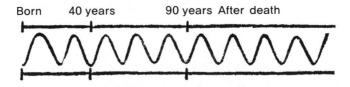

That mind is a dream. It is hell. It is a dream which is an illusion. Man lives in an illusion just as dreams exist but dreams are illusions that never exist in reality. Man cannot live as the Truth unless he is reborn as the infinite Soul and Spirit that created the universe, the everlasting Truth. The Eight Levels of Maum Meditation is the method to become the Truth.

The Eight Levels of Maum Meditation

World of Illusion

Original Universe

World of the Truth

Level 1	Mind		Knowing I'm the Universe
Level 2			Knowing I Don't Have Mind
Level 3	Body		Knowing the Universe is Within Me
Level 4			Knowing the Body and Mind of the Universe
Level 5	Seeing and Knowing		Seeing and Knowing the Body and Mind of the Infinite Universe
Level 6			Seeing and Knowing the Kingdom of Heaven
Level 7	Becoming and Being Reborn		Becoming the Body and Mind of the Universe
Level 8			Being Reborn as the Body and Mind of the Universe in the Perfect Kingdom of Heaven, Receiving the Seal from God on the Forehead and Throughout the Whole Body, and Getting Enlightenment to be Complete

In order to be reborn as the energy and light of the universe which is the everlasting Soul and Spirit of the infinite universe:

I must first eliminate my body, mind, and even the universe.

Then only the Great Soul and Spirit remains. When the Great Soul and Spirit becomes myself, I am reborn as the Great Soul and Spirit.

I, myself, the Truth, become the stars, the sun, the moon, the earth, all creation and mankind. Everyone becomes the Truth and lives forever; this is the kingdom of heaven.

This is the Eight Levels of Maum Meditation. It can be represented in the following illustrations;

When you eliminate individual body and mind from the universe, and get rid of the sun, the stars, the moon, and the earth as well, only pure emptiness remains. This Great Soul and Spirit of the universe becomes you. You are reborn as the Great Soul and Spirit of the universe. This is the everlasting kingdom of heaven.

Imagine that right now, where you are, an earthquake broke the crust of the earth below your feet and you fell into the hot magma under you. What would happen? You would cease to exist. But the universe would still exist; still remain the same just as it is. When you become the universe itself then you can live forever as the universe.

That is the way one reaches perfection, which is the completion of man and which transcends all religions. This is the world beyond the world and is the perfect solution for the future that goes beyond all religions. All mankind becomes one and everyone becomes I, myself. Everyone will live for others and become the Great Soul and Spirit itself, which is the energy and light of the everlasting universe. Everyone will live eternally without death. The reason why man is born into this world is to be reborn as this Being, the Truth.

God created the universe and all beings as perfect. However, man is dead because of his delusions. One must be freed from this and return to the perfect creator. This can be achieved through Maum Meditation. The Soul and Spirit of the universe is living. When one becomes the wisdom itself, of the Great Soul and Spirit, he is able to see and know all of the world truly as it is. Man becomes a saint and will live in this true world, which is the Truth, forever.

The completion of all religions is achieved when we throw away our selves. When we throw away our selves and become the Truth, mankind becomes complete. People should not blame others. Instead, people must throw away the sinful self and become the Truth. Now is the time of the universe and only one who becomes complete can live in heaven. We should live in heaven at this very time.

If one does not become the Truth, he lives being dead in the dream-like, non-existing illusion. If one becomes the Truth, he lives in the world of the Truth forever as the Truth. Maum Meditation is a choice between life and death. What could be more important than saving oneself from death? There is nothing more urgent than this.

It is absurd to believe that a person who is not reborn in heaven while living can go to heaven after death; he can't go to heaven. When one's consciousness becomes one with the Great Soul and Spirit of the universe while living, he lives in eternal heaven forever. It is completely unreasonable to say that one who is not reborn in heaven while living can enter heaven after death.

To say that you can go to heaven when you believe means that you have faith in entering heaven when you have heaven in your mind.

CHAPTER 2
WORLD BEYOND WORLD

The Time for Human Completion

For a human being to achieve completion means that one is rid of sins and is reborn as a child of God. Those who are rid of the conceptions and habits that constitute their self and are reborn into God or Buddha, which is the Almighty God of the universe, are those who have become one with God. They are the children of God. Human beings are the children of the Truth. Living righteously by seeing and hearing truly because they are the Truth is human completion, and completion is to accomplish all. To accomplish all is to become the eternal Truth.

He who has become the eternal Truth has the kingdom of God or Buddha within him. He is God or Buddha itself and the whole and individual is the Truth itself. All that exist live, and this earth and world is the individual himself who has all within, even after his individual body disappears.

This earth becomes heaven, and man lives in bliss where there is no life and death because there is no death even when the body dies, and man lives eternally in heaven. Those who are complete are those who know that this earth is heaven.

For those who are complete, this world and the world after death are not separate, but one. True freedom is to live as it is without judgment and discernment, to live life but not belong to it, and to live absent of one's self. To live absent of one's self is liberation. He who has reached completion has no sin or karma because his self does not exist and he lives eternally in the perfect world. He who has reached completion has no suffering and lives in a peaceful state because his self does not exist. Because he is absent of his self, the mind of all creation does not exist for a person who has reached completion. But, at the same time, everything does exist so that he lives accumulating his fortunes in the kingdom of heaven. Completion is to live without the mind of attachment, which is the mind of an individual, so that everyone is one. Completion is to embrace everyone with a big mind and to live for others.

Now is the time for everyone to live as one, as all. Our world becomes the one kingdom where there is no separation between you and me and where others are put first. The time has come for this world to be heaven. Now is the time for human completion.

ETERNAL HEAVEN

People believe and say that the eternal heaven can only be entered once one dies. The ultimate goal of all practicing religions is to live eternally in heaven after death, and many people believe this to be true. The everlasting Truth of the universe is actually the emptiness that existed before the universe, before the emptiness that we know of. This in itself is God or Buddha. It is known that everything appears and disappears from this emptiness. Because this emptiness is the Truth itself, all things that come from it are the children of the Truth, thus the children are the Truth.

Only one whose consciousness has reached the state before the infinite universe has eternal life and heaven. He is one who is reborn as one with God or Buddha. He is the Truth. He is one as it is without being individual or whole. Within him, all things are living and he lacks nothing. As God is living, all of creation is the Truth itself. Everything is living just as it is.

God originally created a perfect universe. Being perfect means that all creations were allowed to live. Perfection is the Truth; it is God. The Truth and God means to be living and to live.

From the viewpoint of the universe, the whole of creation lives eternally and is heaven. However, he who lives within himself lives in his own delusions which is not reality but death. He lives in his own grave. One who has heaven within himself is one who has died and has been reborn as the infinite universe. For a person to live means to live because he has consciousness. That consciousness is God. God knows, judges, distinguishes, and discerns. Heaven is the kingdom where everything lives forever. It is the world that is one with God or Buddha and is the supreme and greatest world. It is the eternal and everlasting kingdom of heaven.

CAN ALL RELIGIONS REACH COMPLETION?

Religion is the following of teachings. All religions deliver and teach words of the Truth. Now the time has come, when, through the absolution of sin, everyone can become the Truth, the Truth that we have only heard of. When we become perfection itself, there is no separation of different religions. And in turn all religions become one. Through absolution, the ultimate goals for all religions will be achieved as we, who have only heard about the Truth, can now become the Truth.

Who is a Saint?

A saint is one who does not have his individual self but has become one with the Truth, which is God or Buddha.

God or Buddha does not have an image, yet there is nothing in the universe that is not God or Buddha. Everything is God or Buddha in and of itself. Although this is true for all creation, man is not able to become one with God or Buddha. This is because he lives in himself due to his own karmic sins. A saint is a person who is reborn from his grave where he was trapped by living in himself.

The time has come for all mankind to become saints, to be complete human beings. A saint is one whose self has completely died to become the living Truth.

What is the Mind?[1]

The mind consists of 'true mind' and 'false mind.' The true mind is the Truth, Buddha, God, our true nature, or Han-eol-nim[2]; all of which is the original state before the existing universe. The false mind consists of our memories accumulated through our lives and our bodies that store those memories.

---

1 Throughout this book, the English word for 'mind' is used to translate the Korean word 'maum.' Although both of these words generally have the same meaning, the Korean word 'maum' has a broader translation - not only does it refer to its literal English equivalent of 'mind,' but it also refers to 'heart' and 'spirit.' Therefore, whenever the words 'mind,' 'heart,' or 'spirit' appear in this book, the reader should understand the full meaning of the word 'maum.'
2 Han-eol-nim is a Korean name for God that translates to the mind and body of the universe.

How to Cleanse the Mind

The mind must be cleansed because we have the false mind. In Level 1 of Maum Meditation, we eliminate all the life we have lived and are enlightened to the fact that we are the universe, God or Buddha. Being enlightened is the same thing as hearing an answer from God to a prayer.

In Level 2, we are freed of our own ideas of what we deem ourselves to be so that there is no false mind within. This results in the enlightenment to the fact that the inside and outside of ourselves are one, meaning the universe and we are one. We know we are rid of the demons within us.

In Level 3, as we eliminate our bodies in our minds, we eventually come to know that the universe is within us.

Level 4 is about seeing the body and mind of the universe. This is the body of God or Buddha and the mind of God or Buddha, or the Holy Spirit and Holy Father.

Level 5 is about becoming the body and mind of the universe and realizing the meaning of the phrase "Above the earth and under the heaven, only I exist." After we eliminate the self within and are reborn as the one God, which is God or Buddha, we are enlightened to the eternal and everlasting heaven, which is Level 6.

In Level 7, the self is totally eliminated and we become the universe itself and are reborn. In Level 8 we live a life of heavenly bliss, which is the universe. We live on this earth which is heaven. This earth becomes the world of God or Buddha. For all of the above, we must receive the answer from God to prayer. It is not to merely know, but rather, to be enlightened.

The Messiah and the Ascension

The Messiah of the Second Coming refers to Jesus Christ, who is to return one day. Jesus Christ does not have the same image he had two thousand years ago, but is the God who existed before Abraham, the living Christ. He who is reborn as God is the Messiah.

The coming of the Messiah from the sky or heaven is the coming of a person whose consciousness is as high and as wide as God's. The Ascension does not mean that we will rise unto heaven, but those whose consciousness is as high and as wide as heaven, those who have become heaven itself will enter the kingdom of heaven. The kingdom of heaven is not a place where one comes from or goes to. A person whose consciousness is one with God or Buddha and has been reborn as the Truth is one who has ascended. That person is one who has come from heaven.

PRAYER

A prayer is something a person offers in order to become one with God or Buddha or *Han-eol-nim*. To become one with God, a person must cleanse their dark, unclean mind. This cleansing is the absolution of sin.

SIN

Human sin consists of original sin and personal sin. Original sin is inherited from birth. It came to be the moment Adam and Eve ate the forbidden fruit. This does not mean that a tree of the forbidden fruit actually existed, but the discernment by humans between right and wrong and the subsequent sin of holding that discernment in their mind is expressed as 'having picked the fruit and eaten of it.' This discernment caused Adam and Eve to be sinners, like demons. Then they gave birth to descendants who were sinners as well. This is why we are sinners and why we live like demons also. This is the original sin and the sin of inheritance.

Personal sin is the life we have lived as sinners. When we eliminate the self within us as well as our lives and offer up all we have, we are reborn in heaven as the children of God.

To Believe in God or Buddha

To believe in God means to believe the Truth. To believe the Truth means to believe in the Truth that is righteousness. To believe in what is true means to become the Truth. To become the Truth means to become complete. To believe in Jesus means to become Jesus. Those who have become Jesus have faith in him and answer with their mouths. This means that those who confess with their mouths that the Truth is inside them shall enter heaven.

Jesus is the Truth, and those who have not become Jesus cannot enter heaven. The problem with Christianity today is that it puts its faith in the Jesus who died two thousand years ago and refuses to believe in the living God, Jesus Christ. Not seeking true absolution of sin is another problem.

To believe is to become one with what we put our faith in. In order to become one we must pray for forgiveness, then we can enter the kingdom of eternal heaven.

Hearing God's Voice through Prayer

A prayer is something one offers in order to become one with God. The act of prayer itself is the act of becoming one with God. To become one with God means that we must be absolved from sin. When we are absolved of our original and personal sins, we can become one with God. Also, the more we are absolved from sin, the more we are able to hear God's voice. Those who are truly absolved will hear the voice of God. Only when God replies, are we reborn into the kingdom of heaven while living.

Seeing one's True Nature and Becoming It

Seeing one's true nature and becoming one's true nature are not the same. To see it means to merely see the Truth, whereas becoming it means to actually live as the Truth itself. Seeing it and becoming it are as different as the sky and earth. One can only attain eternal heaven when he or she becomes the Truth.

Enlightenment and Hearing the Voice of God or Buddha Are One and The Same

Enlightenment is knowing by the mind within. It knows from within because that mind is true and is God or Buddha itself. This 'knowing' in the true mind is the same as hearing from God or Buddha.

Absolution and Cleansing the Mind

S ins consist of both original sin and personal sins. When we eliminate the life we have lived and our sinful bodies, we are totally absolved from sins. Only God or Buddha which is the Truth within can redeem us from sins. Sin is the unclean mind; the unclean mind is sin. They are the same.

Doe[3], the Truth, Han-eol-nim, God, Buddha and Allah

*D*oe, the Truth, *Han-eol-nim,* God, Buddha, Allah, and so forth, are actually referring to the universe before the universe. The emptiness of the universe is the Truth. This universe is eternal and everlasting, and all such different names describe the universe before the universe. The body and mind of the universe is also called *jung* and *shin,* or the body of Buddha and the mind of Buddha, or the Holy Spirit and Holy Father. The universe is made up of the Great Soul and Spirit. These are all names of the universe.

---

3 'Doe' in Korean refers to the path or way of enlightenment, or Truth. The word is also used to refer to the Truth itself.

ACCOMPLISHING DOE AND REBIRTH ARE THE SAME

Accomplishing *Doe* and rebirth are the same. *Doe* is the Great Soul and Spirit of the universe which is the Truth. He who is reborn as this Grand Spirit and Soul is the one who accomplishes *Doe*. He is a child of God and is born into eternal heaven.

THE FUTURE OF MANKIND

The future of mankind is truly heaven on earth. Heaven on earth is the place where everybody is free and liberated because this world lives according to nature's flow. Therefore, everyone lives for others without self, rejoicing in the happiness of others. Everyone is one.

Because the false mind has ceased to exist, everyone is good, and there will be no thieves. Everyone will know that life and death are one, and so no one will mourn. With the resolution of the conflicts within us and between us we will live happily together. People will have wisdom, thus science will be highly advanced. The rejoicing of mankind will never cease. Because self no longer exists, everyone will live equally, and it will be a paradise on earth for all. Even though our bodies may disappear, people will know we live eternally as it is. Hence, funerals will be held with smiles. It will truly be heaven. Man, having been freed from his sins, will build a great nation of 'oneness' where you, I, and everyone will all be one. We will live a life of nature's flow without a need for laws.

ACCEPTANCE IS THE GREATEST IN THE WORLD

The person who insists that only he is right does so because that person is small-minded. He who insists that only his religion is righteous cannot see the bigger picture because he is attached to his religion. He also is small-minded. A big mind accepts everything. It must be big for it to be able to accept everything.

When Jesus Christ said to be always thankful for everyday life, he meant for people to think positively. Those who think positively are able to accomplish their will. A person who has negative mind cannot accomplish his will in his everyday life. The greatest mind is one that can accept everything. That mind without boundaries is able to accomplish anything and everything. Cleansing the mind completely is the best way for one to be able to accept everything. We are accepting to the extent in which we are cleansed.

EVERYTHING IS ONE

When the God, who existed before this great universe, created heaven and earth, He created it to be complete. Being complete means that all creation lives because all creation is the Truth itself. Everything is one with God as it is. Everything is one as it is because everything is the Truth, eternal and everlasting, knowing no death. It is the Truth simply as it is. It is heaven just as it is. Because it is one, all creation lives and because it is one, everything is heaven.

The Creation of Heaven and Earth

Heaven and earth were created by the will of God. The will of God does not exist per se, but if we had to put it into words, heaven and earth were created by nature's flow. Because this one exists, that one comes forth. Everything appeared by nature's harmony. Everything in heaven and earth exists by nature's harmony and we call it creation. In the Bible God created by his Word (Logos); that Word is God's fundamental nature. This fundamental nature is God. Thus it is said that the creation is done by God.

The Secret of Rebirth

Resurrection means to be reborn as God. Man must be absolved of his sins to be reborn as God. He, who has been completely absolved of sins and reborn as God, and therefore born into heaven, has been fully resurrected.

The secret of rebirth is to be reborn as God without self. The key to this secret is absolution of sin. Only those who are absolved can be reborn. True resurrection is when God acknowledges that all our sins are gone.

GREAT FREEDOM AND LIBERATION

Freedom comes when the 'self' no longer exists and one has become God. True liberation also comes when the 'self' no longer exists and one has become God. Freedom and liberation is for those who are set free from their delusional thoughts and have become one with the one God.

LIFE IN HEAVEN

A life in heaven is the life of God, the Truth, without self. The life of God is a life of nature's flow, a life of freedom, and a life of liberation, and it is the fourth dimensional world. That world is truly heaven, for it lacks nothing. It is where all can rest deeply and just live life as it is.

CAUSAL ACTIONS AND RESULTANT EFFECTS

E verything exists because of 'cause and effect.' The cause is the condition that brings the result. Because a condition exists, there is a result.

A person without money will have money if he works hard. The cause here is working hard and the result is having money.

When there is no cause there can be no resulting effect. That is how you can be free from the cycle of causal actions and resultant effects. Those who have cleansed their minds are free from this cycle, which means they are no longer in it.

ON BEING GOOD-NATURED

For someone to be good-natured means that the true mind lives in him. To say we must be good-natured means we must have the true mind in us. To be good-natured means to have the Truth. When Jesus said that there is none righteous in the world, he meant that no one in this world has the true mind. Being good-natured means to become one with the body and mind of the universe. 'True beauty' is also being one with the body and mind of the universe.

How to Meet God or Buddha

Ｐeople are not able to meet God or Buddha because they don't have wisdom. Wisdom is knowing the Truth; the Truth is God. He who is God has wisdom. When we cleanse impurities in our minds, the true mind will be revealed. That true mind is God or Buddha.

What Are Answers to Prayer?

People pray in churches or temples seeking God or Buddha. However, someone with delusions will hear the sound of their own delusions. They rejoice thinking it is a reply from God. As time passes, they realize that it was the sound of demon which is their own delusion of greed.

When you pray truly by eliminating your delusions within, God or Buddha within is revealed. That is how you can hear an answer to your prayer. The reason God or Buddha within gives the answers is he speaks to us by being revealed as much as we get rid of our delusions.

False Delusional Thoughts[4]

T hose who are not enlightened have false delusional thoughts. Being unenlightened is due to the absence of wisdom. We are filled with demons of delusional thoughts. The external expression of those false delusional thoughts is the present worrying and suffering that we go through. We fuss and fret over whether something is right or wrong according to our own experiences. The wise live in great peace as it is, with no delusional thought.

---

4 False delusional thoughts are mental functions such as passions, afflictions, prejudice and whatever other expression of emotions one may undergo. In short, it refers to any mental function that disrupts and pollutes the mind and body.

The Normal State of Mind[5] Is Doe

The normal state of the mind is *doe*, which means simply living life 'as it is.' *Doe* means living constantly with the same mind. Asking a Buddhist monk on his death bed "Are you the same?" is to ask him whether his mind is the same now as before, as he is dying now.

The true, normal state of mind is the mind of God, the universe. It is the mind of pure emptiness, absent of life and death, without the discernments of what is and isn't. This mind is the one that is constant and always remains as it is. It is God, the mind of the great universe. It is the mind one attains by returning to the mind of God.

---

5 'Normal state of mind' is a mind that has continuity and is in equilibrium.

THE CHILD OF GOD

A child of God is one reborn as God. A child of God is God himself. The Father, the Son, and the Holy Spirit are one as the body of Buddha, the mind of Buddha, and the embodiment of Buddha are one. A child of God is one who has returned to the perfect God. A child of God knows no death, is God himself, and is perfection itself. A child of God lives in heaven. Because he is God, he saves people and lives for others according to the will of God. This is the child of God.

The Identity of God

The kingdom of God is the world of a fourth dimension before the word 'universe.' God existed as the universe before the universe we know and God is the creator of the universe. Complete emptiness is the body of God and within that body exists the one omnipresent mind of God.

The Bible says that Jehovah stands above the wind, which means that God exists before the wind. The state before the word 'universe' is the state of God. The creator of the universe is God and every single creation is the manifestation of God. Even though there exists only one God, there are many different creations. This is because every creation is the manifestation of the one and only God, but appears differently according to condition.

THE LIFE OF A *DOE-IN* (DOH-EEN)[6]

People tend to have their own ideal images of what an enlightened person is. I was asked to appear in some special television interviews at Korean TV stations in the U.S.A. When I went to the broadcasting stations, the staff members there frequently commented that "We expected an elderly person with a long beard wearing a robe that blows in the wind. You, however, are much younger and do not look like a *doe-in* (an enlightened person)."

In the past in Korea, a *doe-in* was someone with many skills or talents, capable of doing things ordinary people could not do and being praised on how great they were. Some people come to the Maum Meditation Center to become a *doe-in* with such fixed ideas and preconceptions. The Center simply advises them to eliminate and discard themselves. Since this does not fit their greedy delusional idea of a *doe-in,* some of them end up leaving.

A *doe-in* is one born again as being one with God or Buddha, which is the everlasting Truth. Just as man can not fly because he does not have wings, everything is the Truth as it is. He who lives liberated is a *doe-in*. He who knows that life and death are one, he who has been reborn as God or Buddha, and he who has heaven in him is a *doe-in.*

---

6 An 'enlightened person' or 'doe-in' is one who is practicing 'doe.'

A *doe-in* does not exist in images. A *doe-in* can only recognize other *doe-in* when he becomes a *doe-in*. This is because a person with lower consciousness level cannot recognize a person with higher consciousness level, for he only sees in his own viewpoint. Only *doe-in* can recognize other *doe-in*. A *Sin-sun*(shin-sun)[7] cannot be recognized by ordinary people. This means a *Sin-sun* is human but people cannot recognize that he is a *Sin-sun*. The life of a true *doe-in* is saving, acting, and living for others. This is a true *doe-in*.

---

7 When man becomes one with God then God appears as man, that entity is 'Sin-sun'. When Sin-sun's body dies, Sin-sun continues to live on. In other words, Sin-sun lives the same before and after the body dies. Sin-sun just lives as Sin-sun.

THE LAST CHANCE FOR MANKIND

The last chance for mankind and the road to salvation is for everyone to be reborn as the Truth, as the whole without self, and to live as one. Mankind will live well when we live as one without separation between you, I, and others and without boundaries between countries. Mankind will live better and eternally as the Truth when everyone comes to realize that everything is his own fault, thus, truly repents and becomes one with others. The discernment of good or bad, this or that, exists because of our own minds. When we are reborn as the mind of Truth and accept everything, mankind will live well.

THOSE WHO ARE REBORN IN HEAVEN
WHILE LIVING WILL LIVE FOREVER

B oth heaven and the Truth exist within us. Those who have not become the Truth while living live in their own delusional thoughts, not the Truth, and eventually die. Only those who are the Truth live because they are the Truth. They can live because they have heaven within while living. Those who do not have heaven within live in hell with pain, for it is death itself.

Both Life and Death Are One

Those who have completely died while living are reborn as the children of the living God. Just as we discard worn out clothing so can the soul discard a worn out body and live just as it is, thus life and death are one. Those born again as the Truth while living do not die but live simply as it is. In the lower levels of enlightenment some people say that nothing exists after death, such people remain in the hell of nothing forever. But for those who live, because their consciousness is awake, this life and the life after death are one. This means both life and death are one.

The Meaning of Confessing with Our Mouth

Religion today declares that with mere faith one can go to heaven. However, no one seems to understand the true meaning of faith. Faith or believing means to become one with that which we bestow our faith in; it is to become faith itself.

For example, he who believes in Jesus Christ must become Jesus Christ in order to enter heaven. He who confesses with his mouth that Jesus Christ, the living God, exists in him is born again in heaven. Only he who receives the acknowledgement from the God within, that God lives in him, may enter heaven. That person is the Truth itself and because he is the Truth, he will have eternal life. Because he is the Truth, he will have heaven and live.

To merely speak the words, "Do you believe in Jesus Christ?" and reply "Yes, I do.", is not enough for a person to be reborn into heaven. True faith is allowing Christ to dwell in oneself, and confirming that fact in our mind and confessing God's existence with our mouth.

The Meaning of "I Am the Way, the Truth, and the Life. No One Will Enter Heaven Except Through Me."

B eing one is the path we must take, and that in itself is the Truth, and that is the life. He who keeps the God before the universe in him will be born in heaven. He who has God, the Alpha and Omega, in him will live in eternal heaven. The way we should take is the state of God before the universe, which in itself is the Truth, and the master of consciousness. Because God knows life and death, God is 'the life' itself. This means, unless we become the true Jesus Christ, we will not be born into heaven.

UNFORGIVABLE SIN

M an has two kinds of sin: original sin and personal sin. He who is absolved, however, is born again and lives as a child of God. Unforgivable sin is denying the true Jesus Christ who is God, which eventually leads to death. This is man's only sin. He who denies the Truth, cannot be the Truth, and only ends in death.

The greatest sin of all is that of not believing in the Truth. A sinner is like one who is confined in prison, unable to be free, unable to do according to his will. That is why a sinner lives in hell even after death. Hell is where those delusional thoughts live on in the burden of suffering. This too is not the Truth; it is death.

WHERE WE COME FROM, WHY WE LIVE AND WHERE WE GO

M an comes from the universe, lives in the universe, and goes back to the universe. Why do we live? We live to accomplish human completion; to be born in the ever-eternal kingdom of heaven in the great fortune of the universe. When we understand the meaning of life, we are reborn as the Truth and achieve human completion. Only then will we enter the kingdom of heaven.

The Difference between Those Who Have Cleansed Their Minds and Those Who Have Not

In the Bible is the verse "Blessed are the poor in spirit for theirs is the kingdom of heaven." To be poor in spirit means to have no false mind. False mind or human mind is a mind full of having and wanting and cannot enter heaven.

Those who have cleansed their minds receive an approval from the God within to go to heaven while living. This world becomes heaven, and we live in heaven while living and continue to live in heaven even after our bodies are gone.

Those who do not cleanse their minds live in their own delusional thoughts. Since such thoughts are not the Truth, not real, it only leads to death. Not only do such people suffer from their burdens while living in this world but also suffer after death in the agonies of hell.

The Meaning of "Repent, For the Kingdom of Heaven is At Hand!"

Repentance refers to the elimination of one's lived life, or personal sin, as well as eliminating oneself, which is the original sin. Those who eliminate both will enter the kingdom of heaven.

The Meaning of Salvation

E ven though everything of this world is in heaven just as it is, man is not able to enter heaven due to his sins. Therefore, salvation enables man to enter heaven.

When God brought forth all creation, it was the complete Truth; it was God. Every creation is a child of the Truth. The Truth gives birth to the Truth to live. Man's sins brought him to death. The absolution of those sins is accomplished through Maum Meditation.

The Legend of *Dan-Goon* (dahn-goon)[8], The Founding Father of the Korean Nation

Long ago, garlic and mugwort were given to one person from the Bear tribe and the Tiger tribe. They were to eat them and were to live in a cave for one hundred days. The Tiger could not endure the days and eventually ran out of the cave. The Bear, however, endured the one hundred days to become human and married *Hwanoong*. From this union *Dan-Goon* was born. This story pertains to Maum Meditation as well. Only those who are like the Bear can reach up to the eighth level of this practice, and those who are so quick and talented like the Tiger cannot endure hunger and suffering.

The process of Maum Meditation can be compared to that of raising a silkworm. Before the silkworm crawls up a prop or a stick in order to spin its cocoon, it eats as much as it can and sleeps. This involves much time as it repeats this process four times. When the silkworm in the cocoon completely dies, only then can the moth be born and come out of its cocoon to lay its eggs. This process is similar to Maum Meditation. It seems that those who are willing to patiently endure are rare in this world.

---

8 The Dan-Goon legend was passed down for generations. It is a story of how the Korean nation was founded.

WHY THERE MUST BE A UNION OF GOD AND MAN

O n the day when God and man become one we will no longer see things through our individual delusions of religion, ideology, philosophy and knowledge; but rather from the completely different viewpoint of God, who is the whole of the universe. To see, act and live from this viewpoint is the Truth; it is righteousness. Man will no longer be ignorant, for the delusions we once believed in will be brought to light as falsehoods and everyone will live with true wisdom. Heaven on earth will be built, for all will be reborn as the Truth, be one, and live joyfully. Because we live selflessly for others, neither thieving nor robbing will exist and we will live our lives with the greatest of freedom. Man will have reached completion, and there will be no death. This world and the kingdom of heaven are not separate but exist as one. Because man will live as the Truth itself, it will truly be paradise on earth.

Conversing with God or Buddha

In this world, it is rare to find a person with true consciousness.

He who has totally eliminated himself and has been reborn in heaven may have freely flowing conversation with God or Buddha. An answer is received at will when one calls for God within him. Anyone who has reached this level of consciousness is capable of a perfectly free conversation with God. A true consciousness is God or Buddha itself.

THE NEW HEAVEN AND NEW EARTH

When the consciousness of mankind is perfect, a whole new heaven and new earth will exist in our mind. The original universe was created in the state of perfection because God, who is perfect, created it. When we see from the viewpoint of God, who is the whole, the universe is perfect heaven, paradise from the beginning. But if man cannot enter there because his consciousness is not one with God, then what is the point of heaven?

The new heaven and new earth has come now, for man is able to have heaven in him. It is the same heaven that has always existed, but because man is reborn into it, this is the new heaven and new earth to him.

In the Bible is the verse, "Your kingdom come, Your will be done on earth as it is in heaven." This means that from the beginning everything has been perfect in heaven and of eternal bliss because everything lives as the Truth. But on earth mankind is dead due to karmic sins. This verse is asking for fulfillment on earth as it is in heaven.

When the self no longer exists in one's consciousness, one then becomes God, the heaven, and has eternal life. We can call this heaven, for the whole creation lives. Those whose self dies for God will not die after death but be born in heaven and live. In other words, those who got rid of self because they have sought repentance and absolution of sins will live in the new heaven and new earth.

THE LIVING AND THE DEAD

O nly the living can recognize the living. The dead can- not recognize the living, but the living can recognize the dead.

He whose consciousness is close to completion can rec- ognize those who are dead. Because his consciousness is complete, he can see that which is not complete. This is the same as saying that only God can recognize God. The living ones are those who are born in heaven. Only they are the living.

Only Those Who Are Thankful
and Positive Can Be Reborn as the Truth

Those who are thankful and positive can be reborn as the Truth. The Truth is the greatest and highest. However, because humans are the narrowest and lowest, it is difficult for man to have the grand Truth in him.

I have seen that man can only have as much Truth in him as he has true mind.

In Maum Meditation, those who have practiced up to Level 1 have a mind capacity to that extent; those who have practiced up to Level 2 have a mind capacity to that extent. The limit of their capacity lies in how far they have progressed. Teacher *Jeungsan*[9] once said that if a person is in a place where he should not be, the light of God will remove him. Because there is falseness, or sin, of want and desire in his body, he is far from the Truth. Then, the Truth, God's light, cannot respond to him and his falseness cannot become one with God, thus God's light removes him.

Those who accomplish completion are the ones who are thankful. Acceptance brings about the greatest capacity, and a thankful and positive mind belongs to those who accept. Only those who are thankful because they have a large capacity of mind can be one with God.

---

9 Teacher Jeungsan is a founder of the Jeungsando, which is a type of spiritual practice in Korea.

After having gone through Level 1, man, out of his arrogance, speaks of having reached enlightenment as a result of his own greatness. However, that is all he can have, for he has no thankful mind towards his place of instruction. Only those who are thankful and persistent may enter heaven.

LIVING BY NATURE'S FLOW IS THE MIND OF GREAT NATURE, WHICH IS TRUE LOVE, TRUE MERCY, AND COMPASSION

Nature simply stays as it is, consistently and without a word, even though the wind may blow and rain may pour. Nature just does its duty and gives humans all they need without having any mind about doing it. Just as Jesus said, 'Do not let the right hand know what the left hand is doing,' whatever we do, we must do with no mind of having done it. When we return to Nature, which is God or Buddha, everything we do with no mind is true love. To just do is true mercy, to just do is true compassion, for everything is done according to nature's flow, the mind of great nature. Now is the time of living by nature's flow.

Whatever is done by the mind of God is nature's flow. Now is the time when anyone can be reborn as completion and live according to nature's flow.

THE CREATOR, GOD

T he creator is God. God is the creator. The creator controls everything from the universe before the universe,
which is the world of fourth dimension. Man knows God
only as an entity with a human image. The infinite universe
before the universe we know is the original image of God.
The creator is the Great Soul and Spirit of the infinite universe.

MAN WAS CREATED IN THE IMAGE OF GOD

The Bible says that man was created in the image of God. This means that the mind of man was created to become one with God. There is no place in this universe where the creator, God, does not dwell. The universe itself is the image of the original God. He who has become one with God lives in God's kingdom. The kingdom of God is the kingdom of life and the origin, or source of all energy itself. It is an eternal and everlasting place.

Everything We Hear and Everything
We See Exists Just As It is, and It is the Truth

People think that when the kingdom of God comes, things will be as they presume. They think that only believers will be allowed to live in heaven and they are anxious for prosperity. People also think that when they become one with God they will be able to fly here and there. However, the most fundamental principle of the universe is that things are the Truth just as we see it, just the way it is. Man cannot fly, for he has no wings; in the same way, it is the Truth that a dog, cow, or horse is incapable of flight.

It is the Truth that man is not able to live eternally with his human body. It is the Truth for the dead that they cannot come on a cloud from the sky. It was said that, amongst us, some would come on clouds just as Jesus Christ who returned to heaven. However, a believer in such delusions of what 'coming on a cloud' means would surely end in eternal death; indeed, for the dead to come in such a manner is not the Truth. The human body is the 'cloud' and He will appear in a human body. All other beliefs of things appearing in clouds are only dream-like delusions. We cannot see this clearly until we wake up from those delusions.

Everything in this world is born of conditions, exists due to conditions and dies because of the condition of longevity. Even in the case of human beings, our life span is determined by the limited number of times our cells can divide in our bodies. What we see and what we hear is the Truth just as it is.

The Meaning of the Transmigration of the Soul

It is said in Buddhism that when a person dies he goes through the transmigration of the soul. It is a rotating cycle and this cycle is caused by delusional attachments. He who has strong attachments exists as a human being while living, but transmigrates into many illusions after death, such as a snake, maggot or fly. As a person becomes and lives his own illusions, the Truth no longer remains in him. Such a state is true pain and hell itself.

On Fate

The life we have lived is the cause that leads to the resultant effects. This is the meaning of fate or destiny. The life of a forty-year-old man is like a movie he has made that spans those 40 years. The producer of his movie is himself; the main character is himself; the audience is himself; the only person capable of eliminating this movie is himself and no other.

This man's fate is the life he has lived for forty years, and it is his fate to continue living whichever way he has lived. Only when he escapes from that movie can he live a life of true freedom, liberation, and eternal, everlasting completion.

THE MIND IS NOT 'NON-EXISTING', BUT IT HAS EXISTENCE

The mind is not 'non-existing', but it has existence. The true mind is the universe, which is existent. We think that the universe does not exist for we cannot see it with our eyes. However, this true mind is not 'non-existing' but existent.

When we have a mind as big as the infinite universe, the universe becomes the Great Soul and Spirit; we know that everything came out from the universe.

DOES THE UNIVERSE REALLY EXIST?

He who still has his individual self cannot return to the mind of true existence. He thinks that nothing exists when he does not exist. What is left in the sky when the stars disappear? When the stars are no longer there, we say that there is nothing. Those who have found the true mind know that the great universe, which is the true mind itself, exists. Those who become the universe itself can see the body and mind of the universe.

Nothing exists in the body of the universe, even this 'non-existence' does not exist. Inside this 'non-existence,' we can see the existence of the one and only God filling it to the utmost. When a person's individual self no longer remains and even the infinite universe exists no more, the mind is able to see. He is reborn as the one God of heaven and earth and is the child of God or Buddha. For those who have reached this level, the material and non-material world are one; they know that all creation will live within them eternally in heaven. Those who have become the universe itself have no mind that they are the universe. For them, everything is emptiness, and they have no mind but they know everything. It is the infinite world of inexhaustible treasures beyond emptiness. Those who have reached the state of God or Buddha have a mind, the mind of God or Buddha.

This is the state in which false delusional thoughts no longer exist, for he has the true mind of all creation. He who has delusional thoughts is one who has failed to become one with God. We are reborn from and into the universe. That mind is the mind of the universe, or God - only the mind of God remains. This mind has no likes or dislikes; it has no discernment of right and wrong, for it lives and exists as it is. It knows no death. Though joy is absent in this mind, its joy is at the pinnacle because it lives in bliss having been reborn into the eternal heaven.

Cleansing the Mind Can Bring Health, Beauty and Longevity

When we cleanse our minds illness is no more. We can be our healthiest, most beautiful, and live longer. It is quite common to see people recovering from their illness while cleansing their minds. The image of a person is his mind. Every single creation lives according to how it looks because it has its own image, or shape, of mind.

Frogs live jumping around, and lions live preying on animals because they are made in the image to do so. Even people behave differently according to their image, which is the shape of their minds.

The shape itself is the mind. What is in our minds appears outwardly. Our minds are our lived lives. When we throw away our lived lives, only the Truth, which is true mind, remains. Illness originates from the false mind that we have. The illness is the image of the false mind. When we eliminate our false mind, the internal flow of blood and energy that has been blocked by our false mind is freed, so that illness disappears. In addition, our appearance can be most beautiful because of our comfort in having eliminated our false minds. This is true for our longevity as well. When we do not have our false human minds and become one with heaven, we are released from suffering; we live with the mind of heaven without suffering from judgments, burdens, or stress. Our bodies become heavenly bodies and live with the longevity of heaven. This is our original eternal lifespan.

Good health depends on one's mind. When our minds are liberated and live as the Truth by nature's flow, the blood and energy in our bodies will circulate well and there will be no more illness.

To Live Better and the Most Important Thing in the World

Jesus said, "Man shall not live by bread alone, but by every word that proceeds out of the mouth of God." One of His disciples said to Him, "Lord, suffer me first to go and bury my father," but Jesus said to him, "Follow Me, and let the dead bury their dead." To a man who wanted to follow Him after saying goodbye to his family, Jesus said that one who kept looking back with a plow in his hand would not be able to go to the kingdom of heaven.

Another saint also said for people to lament on another day when the sun sets. People cannot hear this, for they are only concerned about whether there is bread on the table. The most important thing in the world is to become the Truth, for only he who becomes the Truth lives. People whose consciousness is dead live foolishly because they cannot recognize those whose consciousness is living. Becoming a complete being is the most precious jewel in the world. He whose consciousness is living lives a true life and lives better because he has true wisdom. He is able to truly live because he is freed from suffering and burdens.

People often ask how we could live once we have cleansed our minds. Once we cleanse our false minds and only the true mind remains, we live our lives better because we live according to our own capabilities. Because we no longer have our false human minds, we no longer try so hard to save face and we become more realistic. We cannot live well in the delusional thoughts, for they do not carry actions.

PEOPLE LOOK AT THE POINTING FINGER INSTEAD OF THE MOON

We criticize and judge others by our own standards. Some people leave Maum Meditation because they look at me rather than regarding me as the one who teaches the Truth. My aim has been to teach people about the Truth. I pity those who have left Maum Meditation because of my look, without seeing the Truth. The world is the Truth as it is and as we live it.

People think that an enlightened person should have the attributes of a stone statue of Buddha - solemn, silent, and isolated from this world. However, a true enlightened person lives amongst others, but is born into heaven to live eternally, saving mankind.

I do not fit into the standards of such people. Everything is seen through one's own standards. To some, a certain person may seem just a bit annoying, but to others, that same person may be their worst enemy. To see from these different perspectives is one's own mind; it is one's own image. There is a saying: "The eyes are the mirrors of one's mind." This means that all creation is the mind, which is reflected in our eyes.

GOD IS THE MOST WIDE AND THE MOST HIGH

G od, who existed before the universe, is the most wide and most high. When man's self no longer exists and he completely eliminates the great universe itself, he can see the most high and most wide.

God, who created the universe, is the Great Soul and Spirit, and everything is a child of God and manifestation of God. Everything in the universe is the image of God.

To Rise from the Grave

M ost religions would have us believe that resurrection is the revival of the body. Long ago, bodies were mummified to prevent decomposition due to this belief. The truth of the Truth is that all forms of matter in this world have a limited life span and eventually disappear.

To rise from the grave does not mean that the bodies of the dead walk upon earth with restored bodies. One's own concepts and habits are his grave. He lives in himself, and therefore, lives in his own grave. He who becomes one with the Truth lives eternally with freedom; he is liberated from the grave because he is free from his own self. Therefore, resurrection means that one no longer has one's own self, becomes the living Truth, and is reborn as the Truth.

THE PROBLEMS SURROUNDING CURRENT RELIGIONS

I had given lectures to ministers in Georgia, U.S.A. on the problems surrounding current religions.

One minister said that Christianity in current religions has been divided into over 50,000 denominations. I responded to that by saying, because they did not know the Truth so many denominations were formed according to what people understood and interpreted about the scriptures based on their own preconceptions and habits. Another minister told me a current reality is that religions denounced anyone who did not attend their church and considered them to be heretics. The first problem of religions today is that the true meaning of 'religion' is misunderstood. People do not put their faith in the living Christ or Buddha, rather they believe that they can enter heaven by worshipping Jesus or Buddha, both of whom died between two and three thousand years ago. The second problem is that mankind does not absolve their sins. Everybody in the seminar agreed with my point of view about the major problems in the current religions.

Repentance means that we acknowledge our wrong doings and regret them, and such wrong doings are our sins. We live according to our own point of view based on our own delusions seeking God, Buddha, or the Truth with our mouths, without absolving our sins. May all religions come to know that God is a living God and truly repent so that we may all become one.

The Past Life is the Current Life and the Present Life is the Life in The Future

A person's past life is his current life, while his present life is his life in the future. Man lives with what he has in his mind. He also lives according to his standards. He lives as he has lived so far and will continue to live on in the same way. The mind he had in the past is the same with the mind he has now and will be the same in the future. The past, the present, and the future, all become one only when he eliminates his individual mind.

People store in their mind everything they have seen and heard from their childhood. This is what they have in their mind. We live as much as what we have in our mind. When this becomes the mind of God, we will live forever with wisdom, as the Truth, and with no death.

Man Cannot See with His Eyes nor Hear with His Ears

B ecause man lives with his own thoughts and habits, his eyes and ears are veiled; he cannot see nor hear the Truth. I have been saying the same words for seven years, but only now people have come to understand what I have been preaching all this time because their consciousness had not been awakened until now. This is the same for the Christian Bible and the Buddhist Sutras. People cannot see nor hear such scriptures because their true mind is soiled by their false mind. These scriptures are stories of the Truth based on the viewpoint of God, Buddha, the Truth. He who eliminates his false mind is the Truth; he can see and hear the scriptures clearly, and what he speaks becomes the scriptures itself. A person's life is the scriptures, when he has become the scriptures.

Is the Human Body Immortal?

O nto this earth, man is born, lives, and departs. The human body comes to earth due to the conditions of nature, lives and dies within the harmony of the universe. When one has breathed the last breath of life, it is death. A person's lifespan is the limited life of the human body. Although different bodies have different life spans according to the different conditions of nature in which they are placed, they all end up dying. That is the Truth. Since the life span of a human body depends on the inherent limitations in the number of cellular divisions, which is different in different parts of the body, the body's lifetime is limited.

Autumn of the Universe, the Time of Harvesting

The Bible says that the Messiah will come upon earth one day to pass judgment. Those who are heavy with their sins cannot eliminate them and they will die, but those whose sins are lighter will be freed from them. The God or Buddha within us, who sits in the state of the Truth, carries out such judgment. He who hears God's answer lives in the kingdom of heaven.

He who absolves his sins is reborn and lives because he no longer carries them, but those who have sins will die. People believe Jesus will come and judge us just like a judge does in the courtroom. A person who is born in heaven receives acknowledgement from the God within. He will be judged by the absolution and live or die by the absolution. This is what the Messiah does.

TRANSCENDENCE OF RELIGIONS
AND TRUE ABSOLUTION OF OUR SINS

The transcendent religion which goes beyond all religions of this world is the true absolution of our sins. When our consciousness can neither follow the Truth nor become the scriptures themselves, we do not know the true meaning of religion. Therefore, mankind cannot become one and religions are torn apart into a thousand different denominations.

We cannot go beyond religion until we become the true children of God or Buddha through absolution. Whoever becomes a child of God can live in the kingdom of heaven forever.

GOD IS THE ONE GOD AND HUMAN CANNOT BE GOD

In the beginning, God made all creation alive because God is perfect. The whole of this world already has been born in the kingdom of heaven, but only man cannot enter because he is bound by his own sins. Since God is perfect, when man becomes one with God through absolution, he can eternally live in the kingdom of heaven. This means that man is resurrected from his own grave in which he was imprisoned. He is reborn as the child of God. He is the true child of the Almighty God.

The Absolute God, the One God

People always ask me the same question; "How is it that you teach the Truth?" I answer by saying that I have come to this world in this very time of the universe to complete mankind with absolution and make everyone a saint. Just as there is no specific reason why Jesus and Buddha spoke about the Truth, likewise, there is no specific reason why I came to complete mankind.

A person who had eliminated his self while pursuing the Truth asked "Since I have eliminated my self, have I become the universe?" When a person is eliminated, the universe itself becomes that person. This is of the same principle as a coin, which has a picture on one side but not on the other. Whether there is a picture or not on either side of the coin, the coin is still one coin. When I become the universe, the universe is me, I am the universe, it is all one as it is.

Since God of the universe is energy and light itself, he lives as everlasting energy and light, both elements are God. He who becomes this energy and light is God itself, as the whole is in the individual and the individual is in the whole; that is God itself. He, the individual, is God, thus he lives forever. The kingdom of heaven is where everything is living. He who no longer has self changes into this eternal energy and light. Thus, an individual is born as the whole, and the individual lives in the kingdom of heaven.

Those who do not become the energy and light cannot

live because they do not have the living energy and light. The energy is body, and the light lives in the body as one. Both are God and perfect. Being perfect means living and being immortal. The knowing of God is the essence of wisdom. To know the living God of the universe is to know the Truth. In other words, he who has God's consciousness has wisdom. Wisdom is knowing the Truth.

The reason why human beings are superior to all other creations in nature is because they are able to know God and to have the wisdom of God. The more people have wisdom, the better human lives will be. Religions, ideologies, philosophies, sciences, knowledge, and everything in human lives become eternal. This is the perfect plan for man to no longer have suffering and live well.

BUDDHA, GOD, OR THE TRUTH DOES NOT HAVE A SPECIFIC IMAGE, BUT EXISTS WITHIN ME

We must remember that Buddha, God, or the Truth does not exist in a particular image outside of oneself; Buddha, God, or the Truth exists within me. Therefore, man should not idolize God or Buddha but should cleanse his delusional mind in order to see God, Buddha, or the Truth. Let us be reborn as God, Buddha, or the Truth and live in the kingdom of heaven on earth. Let us do the work of heaven by setting free all mankind from suffering so as to accumulate our fortunes in the kingdom of heaven.

GOD OR BUDDHA IS WITHIN US

The universe is God or Buddha. Only when God or Buddha is within us can we know God or Buddha. That is why we say that God or Buddha is within us. When the universe dwells in us, God or Buddha is within. The reason why God or Buddha is not within us is due to our delusions. When we do not have our delusional thoughts, God or Buddha is within us.

WE SPEAK OF ONLY WHAT WE KNOW IN OUR LIVES

We speak of only what we know from our life experiences. What we know is as much as what we have experienced while living. Only God is capable of expelling our demons. Our true self, God or Buddha in us cleanses our body and mind. Only the living God or Buddha who lives within us can expel our demons from our mind. Only God or Buddha can eliminate our false selves. God or Buddha is the owner of life. Whether we live or die is also under God's will. Whoever has the living God within him lives. Whoever does not have the living God within will die, for him God is dead.

In other words, those who have no sin and have been cleansed will live; those who have many sins and have not been cleansed will die. Those people with many sins cannot completely cleanse their sins.

It is Not Enlightenment Until One Finishes the Final Level

S ome people who do Maum Meditation are only able to do it as much as their individual capacity allows.

Level 1 and Level 2 are as different as heaven and earth. The difference between Levels 1 and 2 combined and Level 3 is that of heaven and earth. The difference between Levels 1, 2, and 3 combined and Level 4 is that of heaven and earth. The difference between Levels 1, 2, 3, and 4 combined and Level 5 is that of heaven and earth. The difference between Levels 1, 2, 3, 4, and 5 combined and Level 6 is that of heaven and earth. The difference between Levels 1, 2, 3, 4, 5, and 6 combined and Level 7 is that of heaven and earth. The difference between Levels 1, 2, 3, 4, 5, 6, and 7 combined and Level 8 is that of heaven and earth. He who has reached completion lives in the kingdom of heaven and does the work of heaven.

Everything is My Fault

When something goes wrong, people tend to blame it on others and resent them. All creation exists because I exist. Therefore, if we found the conditions by which everything came to be, we would find that those conditions are our own faults that are within us.

Because we have hatred within us, we hate others. Everything exists because we exist. When we acknowledge that everything is our own fault and seek absolution then we are reborn into the kingdom of heaven as the children of God.

Blessed Are the Poor in Spirit, for theirs is The Kingdom of Heaven and Blessed Are the Poor at Heart, for they Will See God

When we cleanse our mind, human mind disappears, and we are born into the kingdom of heaven. When our mind is clean, we can see the God within us, just as we can see ourselves clearly after cleaning a dirty mirror.

We can only see God when we become God, just as we cannot see New York City until we are in New York City. The only way to see God and enter the kingdom of heaven is through absolution by cleansing our minds.

Bound and Dead in One's Own Grave Due to Misplaced Faith

People worship their own religions. Since all religions have their own founders, the followers idolize these founders and place their faith in them. People do not understand what the founders truly meant and interpret the scriptures incorrectly, only to end up believing their own misinterpretations. They do not even consider the possibility that what they place their faith in may not be the Truth. Those who are trapped in the scriptures and its founders live in death bound in their own grave. Those who are trapped in their own religions end up dying, but those who do as God says will live. Let us live through true absolution in the kingdom of heaven.

Cleansing Our Minds to Become Poor in Spirit So that the Kingdom of Heaven is ours

Let us cleanse our mind in order to see God and be reborn as the children of God and live eternally. Due to lack of wisdom, man thinks that he can see God and enter heaven only after death. But the truth is, we must see God and enter the kingdom of heaven while we are alive so that it will be the same even after death. Those of us who have not seen God and are not born into the kingdom of heaven as yet; let us all repent. Instead of simply believing and doing nothing, let us repent and become the words in the scriptures.

THE MOST FORTUNATE

People live differently. There are as many different lives as the number of people. Although people live different lives, those who do Maum Meditation in this period of the universe are the most fortunate. Even though there has been an incalculable number of people on earth since the very beginning of time, there has never been a way to enter the kingdom of heaven by cleansing one's mind.

When the time comes for everyone to enter heaven through repentance, it will not matter whether a person has lived life with a lot of resentment or whether a person has lived his life this way or that. What matters is that people who have done Maum Meditation are the ones who have heaven's beauty.

The human consciousness does not know anything, and the difference between the levels of consciousness is that of heaven and earth. Complete man is one who has reached completion. He is the most blessed because he lives in the kingdom of heaven forever.

Jesus once said that a foolish man accumulates his fortune on earth, but the wise man accumulates his fortune in heaven. People who are born into the kingdom of heaven must accumulate their fortune in heaven, then it is the true fortune. One who is born in heaven is so thankful, for it is so wonderful, almost dreamlike. The fortunate, who accumulates his fortune in heaven, will never lose his fortune because he accumulates it in heaven. The fortune is his to accumulate and keep.

When those who are born in heaven accumulate their heavenly fortune while living, that fortune is the Truth. The fortune becomes his forever in the kingdom of the Truth. He who accumulates his fortune in the kingdom of heaven is the most fortunate. The greatest fortune of fortunes is the fortune of heaven. He who is born with the heavenly fortune and further accumulates it in heaven is the most fortunate.

The Delusion that I Am Buddha

While he was practicing the fourth level of Maum Meditation in Korea, a minister once said to me "I think I am Buddha. Am I right?" He asked me this because he had read in books and heard from lectures the phrase "You are Buddha."

Buddha said that you are Buddha when you become Buddha. This means that one can become the true Buddha after he throws away the Buddha in his delusion which says he himself is Buddha. When one throws away the false self and only Buddha remains, then he is reborn as Buddha; he is the true Buddha.

The Form of God, the Truth

People say that what is eternal is the Truth. But if one were asked what the Truth is, no one would be able to answer. The eternal Truth is the universe that existed before the infinite universe. It is the emptiness before the empty space of the universe. It is the state at which nothing exists and even that non-existence does not exist. Nothing exists but God. God exists in the state of nothingness where even 'nothingness' does not exist. All things in creation are appearances of God. Not only the nothingness where even nothingness does not exist is God, but also the consciousness that can be found within this nothingness is God. Although the two are separate, it is all one and the same; it is the eternal and everlasting Truth.

The Truth is the immortal and living God. It exists eternally as it is in the universe without changing. For example, if you place the earth into the emptiness where even nothingness does not exist, the emptiness will neither expand nor contract; it will remain the same. The emptiness exists in its shape, whatever that shape is.

Existence and non-existence are one means that existence is as it is and non-existence is the same as existence. Heaven and earth are one as it is. He who becomes one with the whole infinite universe is reborn as God. Since he is the son of God as well as the embodiment of God, he is the Truth itself. This in itself is the Truth. All creation that does not die but becomes one in the kingdom of heaven is God, the Truth, and therefore, the kingdom is heaven. Getting enlightenment to be complete throughout the whole body is to become one with God, the Truth.

THE CREATION OF ALL THINGS

G od created all of creation. From God all things came forth, hence everything is God's creation. This is God's viewpoint. Everything was brought forth by the harmony of heaven and earth. Everything was created due to the conditions of earth, water, fire and wind. From man's viewpoint this is how all things were created. Knowing that creation occurred of its own accord means to see the individual as God in God's viewpoint. All of the above means the same thing.

We Must Have Righteousness to Live in This World

To be righteous is to be upright; to be upright is to be endless; to be endless is to have no hindrances; to have no hindrances is to have no boundaries. Thus, to be righteous is the Truth which has no boundaries.

Righteousness cannot be found in this world for this world is made by men. Only the Truth can make the righteousness. If all religions, ideologies, philosophies, knowledge, politics, economics, and our entire way of living, were done by the Truth, there would be no hindrances and it would last forever. But because there has been no righteousness, man wastes energy endlessly and lives deceiving his own kind.

The Truth is the only righteousness there is. It is a living Truth. When the whole of mankind cleanses its false minds to live with the consciousness of God, man will live cheerfully in God's light, absent of the burden of suffering. To live in the light of God means to be reborn as God, the Truth, within oneself. Those who live with righteousness are reborn as the light. When man lives righteously he will live cheerfully in God's light as he is reborn as the light of God.

Skills of Doe

When people think of the Truth (*doe*), they think those who have *doe* are able to fly, make things appear out of thin air, turn themselves into something else, and be omniscient, omnipresent, and omnipotent. Some come to do Maum Meditation in order to gain such uncanny skills. For such people it is no wonder that the Truth has eluded them because they came seeking those skills, not the Truth.

When we are faced with a decision to make we would ask ourselves whether the skills of *doe* will assist us in solving the problem. Skills of *doe* are a method achieving *doe*, which means 'the Truth.' Because the method of achieving *doe* is so difficult, man has always wondered if such uncanny skills of *doe* actually exist.

As mentioned before, skills of *doe* refer to the method of achieving the Truth. Man is foolish enough to think that there are people in this world who can fly. If there really were such unusual people, the most they could do with their capability is to win a gold medal at the Olympics. Those who can fly the farthest are the ones who can jump the farthest; those who can fly the highest are the ones who can jump the highest.

The world as it is, the world as we see it, is *doe*. That everything lives according to its own image is the Truth.

LIVING BY NATURE'S FLOW

Living by nature's flow is how the Truth lives. The life of great nature is living according to nature's flow, the life of God or Buddha is living according to nature's flow. So is the life of a person who becomes the Truth.

It is the life in which people live like the flow of water, according to the laws of nature without boundaries, without the separation of others, but as one, living for others without the mind of having done so. To live this way is to live according to nature's flow, working hard with no mind of doing.

EVERYTHING IS DONE ON ITS OWN

Human beings cannot see past the end of their noses because of their 'self.' They cannot see because they live in their own pain and suffering without knowing what life really is. When viewed from the standpoint of the universe, everything happens on its own due to its own conditions.

In this world, everything exists due to causes and their resulting effects. Likewise, when a person works hard to reap what he sows the reward will come about on its own according to how much effort he puts in. Everything happens by itself, it happens on its own, it happens as it is. The whole of nature exists on its own as it is. This means everything exists as it is due to conditions. Everything existing as it is means it exists on its own naturally.

CROSSING THE ARIRYEUNG

'Ariryeung,' which appears in a popular Korean folk song, refers to the name of a crest of a mountain. Finding our true self is like crossing the crest. People think that in order to find something there must be an actual place for us to search. When we say crossing over the crest in order to find our true selves, it means that we must find the God or Buddha within us.

Only those who have freed themselves of their own delusions and demons are able to cross the summit. Only those who no longer have their own selves can gain their true selves.

'Ariryeung' is an old Korean folk song with the lyrics: "My lover who abandons me will not get far because his feet hurt so bad." The verse means that one who abandons his true self no longer has a path to take.

He who has abandoned his true self does not have new life and lives in his own delusional thoughts. This is death. The verse mentioned above is the same as one written in the Buddhist sutras: "Let's go! Let's make haste and go! Over that hill we go!" Furthermore, even the Christian Bible indicates that we will meet after having crossed the River Jordan.

A WORD TO THE LIVING

I say unto the living: Together, let us make this world into the kingdom of heaven! We were brought into this world to bring all creation to eternal life. But the hearts of men have been panic-stricken. People no longer live like human beings, but live selfishly within the confines of their own narrow frames of mind. There is nowhere for the Truth to place its roots and man's own demons pretend to be greater and more righteous than the Truth, so all of this world is false. Only the kingdom of heaven is righteous and no other. So I implore the living, let us gather all our strength to make this world of demons into the kingdom of heaven.

The Will of the Universe

The will of the universe is for all things in nature to live with heaven and earth as one in the kingdom of heaven. But man cannot live in this way because he does not know the will of the universe, as he does not have it within. He who reaches heaven lives the life of the universe and will of the universe. But those who live within individual selves live with their own dead consciousness.

MIND, CONSCIOUSNESS, AND GOD

M ind, consciousness, and God are all one. The mind, consciousness, and God of people that are diseased with delusions are bound to live with delusional minds, a delusional consciousness and a delusional God. On the contrary, those who live with true minds, true consciousness, and true God live with righteous minds, righteous consciousness, and righteous God. In short, the true mind within self is the true consciousness, and the true consciousness is God, which makes them one and the same.

To Believe with the Heart and Confess with the Mouth Will Deliver Salvation

To believe with the heart is for our heart to admit that Jesus, or the Truth, is within us. To acknowledge God's existence and confess with one's mouth is to confirm the existence of the Truth, or Jesus, in one's heart. Those who believe and confess that God exists in their hearts will be delivered unto salvation. Only those who have the Truth in them can know that Jesus, the Truth, exists. To confess with the heart is to hear the voice of God within oneself and hearing it is the only way we can live.

JEWS DID NOT HAVE FAITH IN JESUS

The Old Testament prophesied what would be accomplished in the New Testament, and there will be a time in the future when the prophesy of the New Testament will be accomplished. Even though the New Testament was being fulfilled before them, people who believed in the Old Testament could not see it, and although the foretold Jesus appeared, they did not recognize him for they held faith to the Old Testament.

They were foolish enough to be bound only to what they believed, so they did not recognize Jesus Christ when he came. This will be true for the Second Advent of Christ. Even when the Messiah comes before them, they will not recognize him due to their fixed ideas about the Second Advent of Christ. They are bound to what they have faith in, so they will neither be able to hear the true voice of the Messiah nor be able to recognize Him. They will deny the Messiah. Because they do not know this, the Second Advent is described as "The Lord will come as a thief in the night." Because the Truth comes as a person, they who believe in their own idea that the Messiah will come in a cloud will deny the Messiah. This is because His coming is not as they had thought.

The Bible says that the Son of Man will come and that no one knows when. This means that human beings do not know, but only the Son of Man knows. The consciousness of men is not the Truth, and as human beings, they have eyes that can see Him only as a mere mortal. There is no one in this world whose eyes and ears of the mind are open. This is because only those who are alive can see the living Jesus.

Just as the Jews did not believe in Jesus who walked before them, it was also written in an ancient Korean book of prophecy that even after His coming, those who chanted prayers will continue chanting. Others, who have rung their prayer bells, will continue ringing them. He who is waiting for the Second Advent of Christ, or the future Buddha will keep waiting. He waits because he does not know the fundamental principle that those who repent can enter the kingdom of heaven, as the Bible says "Repent, for the kingdom of heaven is at hand."

The Meaning of
"Thy Will Be Done on Earth as it is in Heaven."

The kingdom of heaven is a perfect world as it is. God created all things in nature as the eternal children of God and they are the same as God. All creation is God as it is. The kingdom of God has been a perfect world from the very beginning. It has been the Truth from the very beginning. It is imperishable. It is the world where those whose consciousness has become the body and mind of the infinite universe live; it is the world of no death. The kingdom of God is the perfect world where everything lives. Because it is where all creation lives, we ask God's will to be done on earth as it is in heaven.

Anyone can live in the complete kingdom when he breaks his chains of sin which have held him imprisoned. That is when the kingdom will be fulfilled on earth.

Is the Repentance of One Who Cleansed His Mind the Same as the Repentance of Other Religions?

R epentance means to be penitent for oneself. It is to reflect on oneself and eliminate his sins to seek absolution. Man's sin consists of the life he has lived and his body. To discard our life and body is to eliminate ourselves completely and this is the way to repent and seek absolution of the sin no matter which religion we believe in. This is true repentance. It is to be absolved of one's sins by completely throwing away the sinner within.

What is Righteousness?

Righteousness is upright, and does not have hindrances, obstructions, or boundaries. It is infinite and the highest and the lowest. A life of righteousness is one free of want, desires, and greed that does not even have a mind of being free of such things. Living by nature's flow is a life of righteousness. Righteousness is the active existence of its own accord, its coexistence with the whole, and the principle that everything lives as it is. He who has become God, the infinite universe, is righteousness. He lives life as God. He lives a life of righteousness.

LET US RECOVER THE ORIGINAL NATURE OF MIND

The origin of the world is the universe before this universe. All things in nature come from the original universe and that is where everything returns. The original universe is the original nature of mind and also the true state of God. He who is reborn as God has everlasting life because he himself is God. He who recovers the original nature of mind lives with complete freedom, liberation, and comfort in the kingdom of heaven.

The time has come for all of us to live according to nature's flow by recovering our original nature. The mind of great nature is compassionate - it is the greatest compassionate love of all. The mind of great nature does deeds without any thought of having done anything. It is a compassionate love that lets all creation live; it is a compassionate love that resurrects. It makes mankind live and sheds light on the whole of the universe. It is to live as one. Mankind lives a life according to nature's flow. If you live a life of the great nature, you live selflessly for others, then your life will get better. Let us all recover our original nature to help the whole of mankind truly live.

We Must Become Religion Itself and Be Free of Sin So That the World Can Become One and Reach Human Completion

He who is bound to sacred books and scriptures of religion cannot enter heaven while living. Only those who have become religion itself may enter. Religion is something that speaks of the Truth, and man will never reach completion while there are religious commandments. For while there are commandments, there will always be sin. One can be reborn into the eternal and everlasting heaven only when he is free from such commandments. He who is free from himself and has become God is free from commandments. For the one who has yet to become the Truth, but is bound to mere words, there is only death. All those who have not become the God of life are dead. He who has become God knows that God dwells in him, and knows that he lives in the eternal and everlasting heaven.

The Truth Is the Origin of Energy and Light and Exists as it is Eternally

S cientifically speaking, the Truth is the origin of energy and light that is eternal and everlasting. It does not wear out, but exists as it is. The Truth exists as it is; it exists of its own accord. It existed before all things in nature were created and exists in them as well. The whole of creation is the Truth itself. Even though the shape of a certain creation may disappear, the shape in itself remains as the Truth. The world that exists before us is the world of the Truth. The individual is the perfect Truth and within the perfect Truth the individual lives; the two are one. It is the eternal source of energy and is energy and light itself. It lives eternally in the world of perfection, the world of the eternal and everlasting source of energy, for it is the eternal and everlasting energy and light itself.

The Kingdom of Light

God is said to be light because he is the Truth, because he is living and he has knowledge of wisdom. God is the original nature of mind, and that nature is living and knows that there will be no death; it knows that God is the master.

The kingdom of God is the kingdom of light. The kingdom of light is the world alive, the world of wisdom; the world of the Truth, the world of life, and the world of God. It is the eternal and everlasting Truth; it is God.

It is the kingdom absent of death, suffering, and sorrow; it is where all creation lives as one. The kingdom is the birthplace of all life and it is where the whole of creation is given life. It is the world where everyone can rest well and live as it is. The kingdom of light is the completion of the material world.

To live means that the Truth lives. One must be the light, God, in order to live. Only the eternal and everlasting God lives forever, but there is no one amongst man who is able to see the living God and the kingdom. This is because man is not poor in his mind. It is because man is rich in false mind that he cannot see God.

All Things in Nature Are the Children of God

All things in nature are the children of God. God is one with the children. God gives birth to the children as the children of God, but mankind does not know God. Men are so filled with their own demons, their own delusions of want, that they are far from God. The kingdom of heaven and God is the same when we are absolved of sin by cleansing our minds. Let us live in the world where God and man are not separate, but one. Let us live in the kingdom of life that is true light.

THE CREATION OF THE BODY AND MIND IS FOR MAN TO BE REBORN INTO A NEW HEAVEN AND EARTH THROUGH THE CREATION OF HEAVEN AND EARTH

People usually believe that the new heaven and earth will be founded in this world, and that dead bodies will be resurrected. However, this is not true. The new heaven and earth will be when the body and mind of man becomes one with God and he builds the new world, the kingdom of heaven, within him. Man is born again by being one with God. This is the creation of the body and mind. This is a shift from the previous genesis of material world to the new genesis of spiritual world. All things in this world of material substance were created by the Truth of non-materiality and the creation of the body and mind is by the Truth of materiality itself.

The creation of the true body and mind is to let human beings be the Truth and live in the kingdom of the Truth that has been alive from the very beginning. This is to live in the new heaven and earth through the creation of the body and mind of the universe.

He who is reborn with the spirit of God is completely one with God. To make God the consciousness of the individual, the consciousness of the individual should exist no more, and only the infinite universe, which is the perfect God of the very beginning, should remain. He who is reborn with the great body and mind of the infinite universe is one who is reborn with the consciousness of God. The state before the infinite universe is the state of God. We are only able to reach this state when our individual bodies and minds are completely eliminated; only then can we be reborn into the true body and mind of the universe.

As long as we have delusions, we will never be able to enter the world of God, the kingdom of heaven. As long as we have delusions, we cannot become God. The next world is where we go after our individual self dies; the world of God is where we go after our individual self dies. Only when we are truly rid of our individual selves can we be one with God.

Completing One's Self Leads to the Completion of One's Life

Completing one's self leads to the completion of one's life. Completion means to have perfectly accomplished eternal and everlasting life. Only the things that have accomplished completion are useful. He who has accomplished completion is useful due to his completion.

With his usefulness, man saves others and lives for others in the kingdom of heaven and such deeds become one's own fortune. It is a life of perfection; it is the world of perfection for man. The perfect world does not die. It is a living kingdom.

The Meaning of the Phrase
"It Will Be Done According To Your Will."

The human mind is of a million different kinds. The people in this world all seem to have a mind of their own. The phrase "It will be done according to your will." means that everything will be done according to makeup of our minds. We do as many delusional acts as we have delusional thoughts in our minds, and the results are as much as the capacity of makeup of our minds.

That Adam and Eve ate the forbidden fruit, the fruit of knowledge means the standards of good and evil were engraved in the hearts of mankind. To do according to one's will, or to have made up one's mind, means to have engraved it in one's heart. Even one's fate is decided by his will.

What is Paganism?

People commonly refer to what they do not believe in, or the religions of others, as being paganism. Buddhism has its own pagan cults, and so does Christianity. However, real pagans are those who do not believe in God or Buddha who is living within them and do not repent their sins.

Those who put their faith in Christianity consider those who do not believe in the Truth, Jesus, to be pagans. This is understandable. However, he who has faith in the living Jesus Christ and repents his sins, is not a pagan.

Faith should not be based upon the wants of man, on prayers asking for one's own good fortune. Instead, we should have faith that God dwells within us, and build his temple in our hearts so as to build the kingdom of heaven. People who are born into heaven because they believe in the God within them and absolve their sins by cleansing their mind and repenting, are not pagans.

THE MEANING OF JUDGMENT BY THE MESSIAH TO COME

It is said that when the Messiah comes, he comes to pass judgment, to separate the sheep from the goats. The trial will depend on one's sins. He who has absolved his sins will live as a winner of the trial; he who has not repented will die as a loser of the trial. He who has repented will live as the Truth. However, one who has not repented will die because he does not have life for he is not the Truth.

What is the True Jehovah's Witness?

That "Jehovah stands on the wind." means that God dwells in the state before wind and that God is the Truth itself. A true Jehovah's witness is he who has become God who stands on wind.

Jehovah is living
Jehovah is the Truth
Jehovah is life
Jehovah is light
Jehovah is the God of resurrection

He who does not simply speak such things but actually helps others become one with Jehovah. He is a true Jehovah's witness.

Let Us Live in the Kingdom of Heaven

Let us live in the kingdom of heaven
Let us stay in the kingdom of heaven
Let us throw away all our burdens
And live in heaven as heaven itself
Let us live in the kingdom of heaven
Through true repentance, through absolution of sin
Let us live in the kingdom where we live as one
Let us live a life as one
Put others before us and
Delight in the happiness of others
Let us live a life of 'us' not of 'me'

Because we are bound to earth, we have suffering and burden. When we eliminate our individual selves that are bound to earth and become heaven, only then can we live in the kingdom of heaven, only then can we live forever. That is where paradise is; that is heaven. In this kingdom of great bliss, all things in nature know no death because they are all the Truth. The kingdom is the source of life, life itself, and lives eternally.

He whose consciousness is not awakened while living cannot be awakened after death. Being awakened means that our knowledge and judgment have become the Truth. He whose consciousness is living lives on, for he is God. God is the one God; only the one God can live for God is the life of God itself.

THE ONE GOD

People believe that there are many gods in the universe, but there is only one. That one and only God appears as millions of different kinds of individual entities, and all such entities are gods. However, such gods are the representation of the one God.

The god that human beings know is that of their own delusions, which is not the true God. The God that has originally existed since the very beginning, the God that is the Creator of the eternal and everlasting material and spiritual world, is the one God. This God is living and eternal; this omnipresent God controls the universe.

The Eyes Are the Mirrors of Mind

Though all of creation is of one mind, the whole of nature is reflected in our eyes. The eyes are the mirrors of the mind since the eyes reflect one's mind. The whole of the existent and non-existent universe is the mind. The mind is one as a whole. Man, however, is deceived by his discernments of what is existent and non-existent so that his eyes cannot see from the viewpoint of the whole. Thus, our discernments of this or that are endless.

Changing one's Mind

W hen we confront a difficult circumstance, people give
us advice that we need to change our minds according to the circumstance. This means to change our viewpoint from that of an individual to that of the whole so that
we are able to think and determine things with the viewpoint of the whole. To see from an individual viewpoint is
to see from our own personal point of view. However, it is
different when we see things from the viewpoint of the
whole for we see with a wider perspective, with a generous
mind.

The Meaning of Having a Generous Mind

To have a generous mind is to have a great mind. It means that one's mind is the whole of the universe. He whose mind becomes the whole universe does not have suffering, sorrow, or pain because he has no individual self. When we have a generous mind, we become of a great mind whereby our small mind no longer exists.

What the Phrase "Heaven Is in Our Hearts." Means

B ecause the mind is the whole of universe, it will be in us and heaven will also be in us if we make our minds one with the universe. Because the Truth, the universe, is within us, that in itself is heaven. He who has truly a generous mind is one who has the universe in him, and he who has the universe in him has heaven in him.

He who has a false mind will always be rich in spirit.
The more falseness his mind has the richer he is in
spirit. He who is poor in spirit means he has true mind and
lacks nothing.

The Meaning of To Cleanse and Empty Our Minds

Our false minds are what we must cleanse and empty. The false mind is not the Truth, which is the whole, but rather the delusional mind of one's own wants. That is why we must work to cleanse and empty ourselves of it.

Both cleansing and emptying mean the same thing. He who cleanses and empties his mind is not chained to anything in life. He is liberated; he is true; he has been born again as the Truth.

What Does the Phrase "Where There Is No Origin, There Are No Seeds; Where There is No Bush, There Are No Branches." Mean?

Everything comes from its own origin and its own seed. We reap the fruit of the seeds that we sow. For example, if we sow the seeds of peas, we reap peas; when we sow the seeds of beans, we reap beans. Likewise, there must be the seed of the Truth for the Truth to exist.

"For where there is no bush, there are no branches." There must be an origin for its presence to exist, just as there is no child without its parents. Present existence and what will come to existence in the future must have an origin in order to exist. One cannot become the Truth unless there exists the origin of the Truth.

The Meaning of the Phrase "Take Your Cross And Follow After Me Everyday. He Who Does Not Fear Dying Shall Live But Who Wants to Live Shall Die."

A cross symbolizes an implement of capital punishment. That we must bear the cross everyday means that we must die everyday. It means that he who truly denies himself and eliminates the individual self within shall be born again as the Truth and live. But he who wants to live shall die because he has his individual self, who is his own demon, and therefore does not have life.

Many people, while in the process of eliminating one's self, are defeated by their own delusions and can no longer throw the self away; hence, they eventually die. He who has completely thrown away his self is reborn with a new life as the living God within him. He who truly dies will live but he who wants to live, or has his individual self, will die.

The Meaning of To Behave According to its Shape

E verything behaves according to its own shape - it lives according to the capability of its shape. This is true for people, animals, birds, and so on. Their shapes are the capabilities of their shapes. Birds can fly because they have wings; lions can prey on animals with their sharp teeth; frogs are able to leap. These capabilities are all due to their individual shapes. Furthermore, different people have different appearances, and such appearances are the shapes of their minds. They live according to their own shapes.

THE MEANING OF "MY HEART IS BURNING."

When Koreans cannot accomplish things as well as they want, they will say that "My heart is burning." This is a phrase they use to express how anxious they are. It means that the mind is like a fire that burns away the Truth. When their true mind is burned up and scarce, people are left feeling restless and nervous.

The Meaning of "It Is Harder for a Rich Man to Enter the Kingdom of God than for a Camel to Go through the Eye of a Needle."

Delusions are the attachments of the mind. Those who have strong attachments cannot enter heaven because of their delusional mind. It is hard for them to get rid of delusional mind due to their attachments. It is easier for a camel to go through the eye of a needle than for a man who is rich in false mind to enter the kingdom of heaven.

THE MEANING OF THE PHRASE
"THOSE WHO FOLLOW GOD WILL THRIVE,
BUT THOSE WHO DISOBEY HIM WILL PERISH."

Those who obey the will of God live their lives by the will of heaven. They will prosper without conflict or hindrance because they live according to nature's flow. However, those who disobey will perish in the end as they live by their own attachments. The former is the living, while the latter is the dead. The living only has additions to their lives while the dead suffers a life of loss.

The living have wisdom, so they live rationally without conflict and always flourish as they live life as it is. The dead remain dead in their own state of delusion. Their dead delusions themselves think they live, but because they do not have true wisdom nor the mind of great nature, they live a fruitless life full of conflicts, only to result in death.

It is only natural that the followers of God flourish in great peace since they have pure wisdom in their lives. Therefore, it is obvious that those who disobey God perish since they live with their own dead wisdom derived from their dead consciousness.

Those who follow God accumulate their fortune in the kingdom of the Truth and the kingdom is filled with prosperity with each passing day. Those who disobey God accumulate their fortune on earth for their own gain, only to perish in the end because they have accumulated none of their fortune in the kingdom of the Truth.

The Definition of Mind and its Presence

W hat man has in his consciousness is called mind. He who does not have the true mind has his own individual mind of delusions that are bound to his attachments. He who has in him the God of the very beginning, the true universe, is the Truth itself. This is the true mind. People frequently say that they no longer have mind because there is no self within, but the true mind is the whole of the universe before the universe.

THE UNIVERSE

The universe also has a body and mind, and only he who is reborn with the body and mind knows it. Only he who becomes the universe itself knows it. It is the place that exists beyond the mind of non-existence. It is the world of inexhaustible treasures; it is the kingdom of God. He who is born again as one with this kingdom is a child of God.

He Who Says He Has No Mind Has Not
Completely Eliminated Himself

He who says that he no longer has any mind is the one who has not completely eliminated himself. He has yet to receive great freedom and liberation. He is yet to be reborn in heaven. He has yet to be free from himself. He has yet to be transformed into the whole, the consciousness of God.

He who only has the true mind, which is God, no longer has his self. He has been transformed and born again as God. Therefore, he is at great peace. He has received liberation. He knows no death and lives in paradise where life and death are one. He lives in the eternal and everlasting kingdom of heaven while living, and therefore this earth is the world of God; this earth is the kingdom of heaven. The life he has lived on this earth continues forever on this earth as the Great Soul and Spirit of the universe, God. Even after his body dies, there is no death.

In this state there is creation; in this state there is rebirth; in this state one is able to see the living God.

The difference between heaven and hell is that heaven is the world of life while hell is that of death. Heaven is a world of freedom, while hell is that of confinement. While heaven is a world of the Truth, or light, hell is a world of delusion absent of light. He whose consciousness is the highest and widest is God, and lives in the kingdom of heaven.

Why Can't Those Who Leave Maum Meditation During Their Pursuit of the Truth Reach the Truth?

B ecause they have their own selves, people mistakenly think that the amount of the Truth they achieved through Maum Meditation is due to their own greatness. Such people do not have a big thankful heart towards Maum Meditation, which guided them towards the Truth. Many people give up meditating because it requires a lot of time to pass Level 4. They think they know the method completely since they were simply told to discard and eliminate everything.

It is not possible for a person who could not complete his meditation at the center to leave and achieve the Truth on his own. At most, if he were to continue meditating by himself, he would be able to maintain what he has, but he would still never be able to achieve the Truth. Such a person has already developed so strongly his own attachments and thoughts of his identity that he is not able to meditate properly. His own thoughts about his identity are his own demon, which has become so big and strong in him that he has nowhere to contain the greatest and highest: the Truth.

As a person is guided by instructors and follows their teaching in times of hardship, his consciousness will eventually be awakened. It takes a certain amount of time to pass in order for a person to be cleansed. To complete even one level, smaller things must be broken down in order for a big breakthrough to occur.

Because man's mind is bound so tightly by sin, and thus

harder than a diamond, when he continuously tries patiently without being anxious, he will eventually be awakened one day.

In the end, those who are not truly sincere cannot achieve. Just as Christianity says that sinners cannot be born into heaven, and Buddhism says that those with heavy karma cannot reach enlightenment, those whose delusions, or demons, are strong and powerful cannot achieve. Even the teacher Jeungsan said that God's light removes those who sit where they should not be sitting. This means that because his delusion makes him far from God, man cannot become God's light, and therefore, he is dragged out from the place of God's light.

Even after passing Level 4, the meditation methods taught in Levels 5, 6, 7 and 8 are different from one another, and therefore, if not for these methods for each level, thousands of people would not be able to pass even one level. Although man may try to be awakened at a certain level as well as try to reach completion in that same level, he is not enough and remains in the same place he was before. The Maum Meditation method as a whole opens one door at a time in order to lead people towards completion.

Until one reaches Level 8, which is completion, he is still curious and has doubts and suspicions; he is ignorant due to his own insufficiency and delusions. He himself knows that he is not complete. He who is complete is not curious about anything nor does he have any doubts or suspicions. He has no delusions for he lacks nothing and knows everything; he is the achiever of all. In this state of completion, he lives as the original God of the universe born into the kingdom of God or Buddha, into the kingdom of heavenly bliss.

Demons

D emons are those who are not one with the Truth.
People think that there are creatures set different from
the rest called demons, but actually the demons are sinners
with delusions. In the previous heaven (see page 139), there
lived a god of want who had not reached the completion of
the Truth. Because such a god lived in the kingdom of heav-
en there existed separation amongst people, the highness
and lowness of ranks. Because such a god dwelled in
people's minds, there existed the separation amongst people
as well as the highness and lowness of status in this world.
Because this was in the very origin of people's minds this
earth is also the world of demons.

This earth, this world of demons, is a place where people
cannot live together as one, where money and social status
are the standards of a person's worth. Because the god in
the previous heaven was not perfect, he could not give life,
and thus, earth has become a world of attachment and
greed, a world of demons. In such a world, man has also
become a demon out of attachment and greed.

Now is the time to drive those demons from heaven and
earth. The time is now for heaven, earth and man to become
one by driving out one's own demon of delusions. It is now
time for the kingdom of heaven to be built on earth and for
man to be reborn as the master of the world.

Oneself is the demon. While one has the whole world in
him, because of his countless demons of delusional

thoughts in him he cannot be reborn as a child of heaven. When the kingdom of God casts out and destroys the demons in man, the kingdom of heaven will be built in the minds of men. Men with the kingdom of heaven inside them will not die for they are the Truth. The demon is the sinner. The demon is death.

This World Exists Because I Exist

This world exists as it is. Because the individual called 'I' exists, the consciousness of the individual, which is God, knows this world exists as it is. Because the 'I' exists, the universe exists. To know the universe and to know that the universe is within oneself is because 'I', which is the universe, exists. The world exists because of 'I.'

THE TRUE MIND

The true mind has no weight
The true mind does not have desires
The true mind is the heaven and earth itself
The true mind is the universe
The true mind knows no time
The true mind exists as it is
The true mind exists on its own
The true mind is the body and mind of the universe
The true mind is
Not bound to birth, age, sickness, or death
The true mind is God
He who has the true mind is one
Whose consciousness has awakened completely
He who has the true mind is God

For a person whose true mind itself becomes the consciousness of the individual, his mind is true consciousness. That consciousness is God. He lives and does not die. He who lives is born and lives in eternal and everlasting heaven. He who lives knows no death; he who lives is one who has died while living. This person no longer has his self and has been born again as the Truth. He lives by nature's flow and works for the deliverance of mankind. He who lives dwells in the world of the living, and his joys are endless. With a grateful heart he lives by the will of heaven; its will is that man lives accumulating his fortunes in the kingdom of heaven.

Man lives according to his mind. He who has a true mind lives in the living world with a living consciousness. He who has a true mind lives, and he who lives accumulates his fortunes in the kingdom of heaven by doing the work of heaven. Such fortunes are everlasting; such fortunes are his. In the living world he lives with his fortunes. He who has fortune lives in the kingdom of heaven everlasting, and the glory of the kingdom of heaven is his.

The Meaning of "Those Who Have Seen God Will Die."

God cannot be seen through the eyes of man. No man shall see God and live. God cannot be seen through the eyes of a man, the sinner. Because God is the greatest and the highest, it takes a man with the greatest and the highest consciousness to see God.

Man is able to find the God in him when he completely discards his own concepts and habits that has bound himself and that has made him a sinner. When man has seen God, his individual self dies for which he is born again as a child of God. Thus, it is said that those who have seen God will die.

THE MEANING OF TO RAISE THE TEMPLE IN THREE DAYS

Seeing a temple, which was still in the process of being built for forty years, Jesus said, "Destroy this temple, and in three days I will raise it up." People may think that Jesus was able to build a temple in three days because he was the Son of God and thus, omniscient and omnipotent. But in truth, he meant that when we repent all of our sins and enshrine God within ourselves, the temple is our bodies.

Jesus also said that not everyone who calls to the Lord can be born in the kingdom of heaven. He who actually follows God's words can be born into the kingdom. God is not in this place or that, but dwells in us. He who throws away whatever fixed ideas and habits that he has as a sinner is the temple and can be born into the kingdom of heaven.

That Jesus Accomplished All

To have accomplished all means to be complete. Completion is to have accomplished perfectly. Completion means to become God and to be absent of death. This means to become perfectly one with God. Jesus died while sacrificing his all for the Truth and in place of his individual consciousness only God remained. Thus, he was born again as the Truth.

This is the eternal God, the Truth itself, and only God lives forever. He who is born again as God is one who has been resurrected.

That our bodies will die one day is the Truth. Even the stars and the moon have their lifespan and so does the earth. He whose consciousness has become God lives eternally on earth; this is the kingdom of heaven. Even if earth in its physical state of matter along with mankind in his physical body were to disappear, the whole of earth with all its creations and mankind would live forever because they are the Soul and Spirit of the eternal Truth, God. He is the awakened; He is the living; He is the one who has accomplished all.

EDUCATION

Education refers to the upbringing of people through teaching. Today's education puts emphasis on what is needed for individuals to live everyday life well. Although the current education can prove to be productive at times, it is inadequate.

Because people lack education in human nature, current education is focused on self-centeredness. A division exists amongst people thus they separate 'your country, my country,' and 'what is mine, what is yours,' and do not learn how to live as one.

A complete education is one that makes man complete. People have said the complete education teaches the values of knowledge, virtue, health and courtesy. But people do not understand the meaning of completion.

Some people say that a 'complete man' is a person with knowledge, benevolence and courage, but this is not the 'complete man.' The 'complete man' means a man who is perfect. The only thing that is perfect is the Truth. When people become the Truth and do research in many different fields, a true study will be established. Everyone will be able to learn it easily. People would no longer have to study the knowledge of delusions. They could then make the world a much better place full of growth and what is true.

Because the Truth does not die, the true studies will flourish. Just living on earth itself would become a true study so a perfect life becomes a field of true study. People would no longer have mental or physical illnesses and they would no longer have to suffer hellish learning, nor would they need to waste their energy pouring over useless studies. People would have their human nature restored and learn how to live as a human. Once people become the Truth, their field of study will be easy and perfect. Those who have become the Truth will have enjoyed their field of study.

The greatest goal of education would be to first study the education of 'complete man,' then to specialize in a particular field. That education would not require as much time and people would be able to receive a perfect education.

WE CAN ONLY OFFER AS MUCH AS WE ARE CAPABLE OF

We can only offer as much as we are capable of offering, just as we can only teach as much as we are capable of teaching. Since I have been trying to teach people boundless Truth, many have been very judgmental. The Sorim Buddhist Temple in China teaches the Sorim's martial art. If there was a person who could breathe fire from his mouth, one could go to him and learn his skill. Likewise, if there was a person who could fly, one could go to him and learn to fly. If there was an all-knowing wise man, one could go to him in order to learn his wisdom.

When a person comes to Maum Meditation, he can become the Truth by learning how to cleanse his mind. Maum Meditation can offer the Truth because it has the Truth; it can teach the Truth because it has the Truth. Therefore, it is natural that only a person who is the Truth himself can teach the way to the Truth.

Saints who have come and gone from this world leave behind their teachings. Jesus left his words of Truth through the Bible while Buddha left his in the Sutras. Just as an English teacher teaches English, a Korean teacher teaches Korean, and a teacher of the Truth teaches the Truth, everyone can teach only as much as he is capable of.

There are so many people in this world who consider themselves a *doe-in*, an enlightened person. A true *doe-in* is one who is God, whose state is that of the universe before the universe, the eternal Truth. He who is not the Truth itself can neither offer the Truth nor teach it. He who has the Truth can offer the Truth and teach it.

In an ancient Korean book of prophecy, it is written that out of a thousand birds there is only one bird of heaven, the Phoenix. The Phoenix refers to the only one who is the Truth out of all who claim to be enlightened.

Those who study Maum Meditation find the true mind, because Maum Meditation has the true mind.

The Completion of Man

For a human to be complete means he has become God. God is eternal and everlasting and exists as it is. The completion of man means that a human being accomplishes perfection, and that means that he has become the eternal and everlasting God.

He who has become God allows all creation to be born into the kingdom of God by God's will, and he himself lives in the kingdom of God.

A person who has reached completion while living will live in the kingdom of heaven even after his body dies on earth. This is the completion of man.

Heaven, Man,
and Earth Are Perfect Only in the Perfect World

The perfect world is a living world absent of death. It is the world of God. It is pure energy and light itself; it is the origin of energy and light, and will never cease because it is eternal. It will be perfect when heaven, man, and earth are reborn in this world.

Perfection does not die. Perfection refers to what has been made complete. Thus, perfection is the Truth as it is and exists forever. When this world is complete, existence will be complete and that eternal existence as it is will be perfection. When all creation is reborn as the Great Soul and Spirit of the universe, which truly exists and is the master of all creation, then the perfection of the world comes true.

The Meaning of "both Heaven and Hell Are an Illusion."

While hell is the realm of death, heaven is that of life. To be living means to be life itself. Hell is the illusion of one's delusions while heaven is the world of reality. Those who have been enlightened of only the non-material world regard heaven as an illusion because they do not know what is real. The whole of existence must live in order for the universe to be complete. Man must live in order for the universe to be complete.

The Mind is not of 'Non-existence' But Rather Existence, And Thus, the World Exists

The mind is not of 'non-existence' but existence. Because of its existence both heaven and earth exist. He who has the true mind, which is of existence and living, will live in heaven and will know no death. The universe is the true mind. The universe consists of both body and mind. The person who has no individual self and has become pure God has no mind, he has the great mind, the mind of the universe. He does not have his own individual mind. It is the mind of God or Buddha. It is the mind that exists as it is with pure emptiness, with no delusional thoughts. It has the body and mind of the universe, so it is the world of Buddha, or the kingdom of God. He who has eliminated everything becomes the universe itself. He who has eliminated everything is born into the eternal kingdom of heaven.

Only those who are written in the Book of Life Will Live

Only God has life. He whose consciousness has become the God of life is recorded in the Book of Life. He who has been completely absolved of sins and has become life itself lives eternally in the everlasting kingdom of heaven. The God of life is true consciousness. He whose consciousness has become the eternal and unchanging God of life lives because he is in the Book of Life. He has gone to the kingdom of heaven.

THE DRAGON[10] FROM HEAVEN

T he dragon appears and ascends to heaven when the gate to heaven is open. The dragon represents the bridge between heaven and earth and makes heaven and earth one. This singifies that a precious person is to be born.

---

10 In oriental culture the dragon is a symbol of benevolence, good fortune, and luck. The dragon referenced to in this passage is a creature who will bridge the gap between heaven and earth.

THE ETERNAL TRUTH IS THE UNIVERSE THAT EXISTS BEFORE THE UNIVERSE

The eternal Truth is the original universe, or the universe before the universe we currently know. The whole of creation must reach this place, the universe, in order to become complete and live eternally. The place before the universe is called the kingdom of heaven in the Bible; it is also called the kingdom of God or the world of Buddha.

This kingdom is complete and exists as it is. This is the kingdom that existed even before God brought forth creation, and the kingdom of the eternal and unchanging Truth even after this world disappears. God brought forth all of creation into this kingdom in a state of perfection. Only mankind remains dead due to his sins. God allows him to eliminate his sins and be born again into the perfect kingdom of the Truth where he will shed no tears and suffer no pain. The life he lives will be the light of God and he will live in the kingdom joyfully.

For a person who has the whole of creation alive in him, this world is heaven. A person who is complete, even though his body may disappear, will live eternally in this world, which is heaven. A person whose individual self becomes the whole, and alive, is absolved of his sins and is reborn as a child of God. When he becomes this, he is God. He himself is God. He lives as it is without death and in absolute freedom and liberation.

Everything lives as it is because it has no sins. Having no sins means that nothing in nature has its own standards about what is good or bad. To have no such standards means that everything can live as it is. Everything in this world is living, but only man is dead due to his sins. I say unto mankind, "Repent your sins so that you may be reborn as the eternal embodiment of Truth and live in the kingdom of heaven, which God created. Let us go live as one in that world where all are one. Only those who discard their sins can now enter this reality, the eternal kingdom, which was once only a mere fantasy."

THE KINGDOM OF HEAVEN

Many people have hoped to go to the kingdom of heaven, which they imagine to be somewhere high up in the sky. However, the kingdom of heaven is inside us and it is the whole infinite universe. We can only enter heaven when our minds become this infinite universe itself.

Entering this kingdom is even more difficult than for a camel to go through the eye of a needle. It is a place where no ordinary man can enter for the sins of man are too great. The kingdom of heaven is in man, and he is the master of that kingdom. There is neither discernment concerning right and wrong nor are there any conflicts or disputes in the kingdom of heaven. He who has discarded all his burden of sins can live in the kingdom of heaven.

One is one's own sin. Only when a person sacrifices his body and his life, which he considered his true identity, to God, can he live in the kingdom of heaven. One has the Truth when he eliminates everything. This is because he is the universe when his self no longer exists. Such a man is God of the universe living eternally as God in the kingdom of heaven without death.

The Life of the Righteous

Jesus once said that he was not a righteous man and that God is the only one who is righteous. Indeed, a righteous man is the one who is reborn as God when his self has completely died.

Man believes that everything disappears when he dies, but this is not true. Even though he may die, the eternal undying universe still remains.

He who eliminates all of his delusions while living dwells in the kingdom of God. He lives in the kingdom as a child of God, with the consciousness of God, whereby the kingdom lacks nothing. A righteous man works for the deliverance of all beings from pain and suffering in the dead world and he accumulates his fortunes in the kingdom of heaven.

Only those who do not have their own minds, whose consciousness is perfect, and who have totally left the dead world, can execute the deeds of a righteous man. Those who are not righteous are ill both in body and mind. Those who are perfect both in body and mind are the righteous ones.

Absolution Is God

The mind consists of the 'false mind' and the 'true mind'. The false mind consists of one's life and body. The false mind is what chains one to his life and body, and because one is bound to his life and body, he is a sinner. Eliminating one's life and body is the same as absolution of sin.

Since one lives chained to his sins, he can recover the true mind when he eliminates those sins. Man has two kinds of sins - original sins and personal sins.

Original sin has been passed down for generations ever since the creation of human beings. The first humans distinguished between what was good and what was bad, and as soon as they put these discernments inside them, the original sin was committed. Our ancestors are sinners, demons. Thus, the children of demons were born as demons. Therefore there is original sin.

Personal sin is the individual's life he lived.

When we cast away these sins, the true mind appears. The true mind is the kingdom of God; it is God itself. The true mind, or God, existed before the universe we currently know and it is the body and mind of itself, the body and mind of Buddha, and the Holy Spirit and Holy Father. It is the body and mind of the universe.

He who has become God is the eternal living energy and light itself.

The energy and light is God, so it lives forever. It lives

eternally in heaven, which is the kingdom of God. Since it is inside man, we simply call it 'mind,' but a person can only have the true mind when he becomes God by eliminating his human mind. Beyond the mind there is God. He who is reborn as God has the mind of God and lives eternally as God.

Enlightenment Is the Voice of God

Enlightenment is achieved when the true mind in us awakens. We know when our consciousness has been awakened. It is when we hear the reply of God inside us. Enlightenment comes when our consciousness or our mind expands bigger, higher, and wider to the extent of the capacity of our mind. Enlightenment is when our dead minds awake and when our true mind, which has been hidden behind our own demons, is freed from its cage. Then we are able to hear God's voice as much as God has been revealed. Because the mind, or consciousness, is released from sin, we are able to hear God's reply according to how free we have become.

When we cleanse our sins and become one with God, God inside us teaches us according to how far we have progressed and we answer with our mouths according to how much we have in our hearts. We confess with our mouth, from our hearts as much as we are close to the Truth. The true mind inside us is what knows, and since it acknowledges as much as it knows, it accepts.

Enlightenment is true prayer, which is the absolution of sin. Since we are released of as much sin as we have sought absolution for, we have that amount of freedom. Our master is God and so the God inside us replies to us as much as we have been cleansed.

When a person has been completely absolved of sin, he is an enlightened being. He has no curiosity, no hindrances and lives in the great freedom. It is a state with no attachments, which existed before the state of emptiness; it has become the mind of God, the mind of the eternal and everlasting universe. Thus, we are free of delusional thoughts. We would be rich in spirit for we have everything, yet we have no mind of having it at all. The rich in true spirit lacks nothing and does not have delusional thoughts. Thus he accomplishes all. When we reach completion, this world will become heavenly paradise because we will not die. Only God will remain in our place and so, even after our body dies, we will continue to live in God's kingdom. He who accumulates his fortunes in heaven working for the deliverance of all beings is a truly enlightened person.

Deeds done by the enlightened person are accumulated in the kingdom of heaven. It is not a dream, but reality that we will live eternally in the kingdom by our own fortunes that we have accumulated. So great will be our joy that it will be dreamlike. He who is completely enlightened works and lives in the kingdom of heaven.

To Communicate with God, One Must Be God

G od is the universe before the universe we know. It is the eternal Truth. The Truth is the body and mind of the universe, the body of Buddha and the mind of Buddha, and the Holy Spirit and Holy Father. The Holy Spirit is the embodiment of all existence; the Holy Father is God, which is the mind of all creation. The origin of all creation also has a body and a mind just as human does. The body and mind is the Holy Spirit and Holy Father. He who no longer has his self is born again with the true body and true mind of the original infinite universe, and that person is God. He who has become God has obtained completion. He who has become God is able to communicate freely with God, and knows all about the world of God, for he himself is God. Man is complete when he communicates with and knows God.

When man has not reached completion, communication with God is self-centered. By misidentifying their own delusional thoughts as God, they hear what they want to believe as a reply from God. But later people may realize the reply from God is false.

In the early days of Maum Meditation, many people who completed only the first level were allowed to communicate with God in the world of true reality, which is the world of God. However, they received answers to questions only as much as they knew, and they talked only about their own delusional thoughts. Since then, I have not allowed that any more and have only concentrated on letting them be God.

God is the highest and lowest, as well as widest and biggest. He who is reborn with the consciousness of God is God as it is. He does not even need to communicate with God to know about God, for he himself is God. The world of God, which is in perfect form, cannot be entered by ordinary people. There are some instances when those who are pure in mind are able to see the world of God. Even in those instances, if they ask self-centered questions it will only bring forth self-centered answers. Only when a person offers his all to God and thus becomes God, can he truly know everything.

CHAPTER 3
THE KINGDOM OF LIGHT

VERSES TO ENLIGHTEN OUR MINDS

The Appearance of the Mind Is Existence

Rain is rain
A cloud is a cloud
The world is the world
Many things are of many things
Everything is a life in and of itself
Everything is of the appearance as it is
For all creation is in me
All creation in me lives
It is the representation in and of itself
It is the absence of death
It is the mind in and of itself
In which it is born again and lives
Existence is to be

Rest to Find and Live the Truth

Weary wanderer, come and rest a while
There is nowhere to go in such haste
Let us think rationally
When you do not know the answer
To the most important question:
"What is the true meaning of why I live?"
"What is the point of your aimless travel?"
Weary wanderer of pain and burden
One who knows
Where he comes from
Why he lives
And where he goes
Lives well
To live your life ignorant of where to go and then die
Is to be in hell and death
The wise are those who know where to go while living
Do not live your life
Like a raving demon absent of prudence
Bound to fallacy as if true
To reflect,
To know and live the Truth
You live eternally in heavenly bliss with no death
This is the fortune of fortunes
And a life of the greatest happiness
If you die reckless and absent of prudence
Your false mind now will be the same as tomorrow

To leave you nothing but fallacy
Discard your life
If you discard your life, there is the life of the Truth
Discard your love, money, and fame
And only the Truth will remain for you to become the Truth
The proud are too proud to discard all
The foolish are too foolish to discard all
You hold fast to your false self
And are saddened, sorrowed; you laugh, then cry
Only to find that it is futile
Bright is the world and the time has come
For all to be born in heaven while living

Come Live in Heavenly Paradise As It Is

Do not come to me in order to know
For I know of nothing
Do not come to me pleading in want
For I have nothing to give
Do not come to me thinking you will gain
For there is none to do so
For I am the great universe without self
I live as it is, I exist as it is
Free and liberated,
I live in heavenly paradise
Eliminate the self
For the self exist no more, only to become the universe
Born again to live as it is
That is where heaven is
That is to live the life of heaven
And that is all you ever need to know

A Life of Heaven

Though flying takes all away
Everything is still in me
Even
The multitudes of pain and suffering are in me
In me, all creation lives
In me, all creation dies

The logical orders of heaven and earth are in me
All forms of creation are in me

Though I live this world
I do not live in it
Though I live life
I do not live in it

Though this is heaven
The dead
Live in hell

Rise from the Grave

He who follows the clouds lives in the clouds
He who follows the winds lives in the winds
He who follows religion lives in religion
Because man lacks wisdom
He continues to live in his environment
He is caged in it
That is where hell is
That is where man dies
That is his grave
Man must come out of it to know what the Truth is
And be free of his burden of pain
It is the greatest freedom of all to live eternally as it is

THE TRUTH

Time may pass again and again
But I live life as it is, absent of death
I exist as it is in the world
I live in the perfect world of God or Buddha
I know no death for I am the light, the Truth
I am the Truth in and of itself
The eternal and everlasting Truth itself
Even before the infinitude of time,
I was
In the infinitude of time to come,
I am
Thus, I exist as it is

Only Man Is Dead

Everything is perfect
Everything is alive
Everything that is, is perfect because
Everything is God

God is all of creation
And non-existence and existence are one
In the image it has become
This, in itself, lives
In the kingdom of God
All is living

Heavenly paradise is the kingdom of God, the living kingdom
Hell is the world of delusions, the dead world

Everything in heaven and earth is living
Yet, only man remains dead

Let Us Cast Away Our Delusions to Live With the True Body and Mind

In my own delusions
I was caged
In it I had lived
I did not exist as I, only as delusions
I did not know that these delusions meant death
After eliminating a million different lives I have lived,
I now know who I am
Since I live in the world of true body and mind
And I now know this body and mind of God
I live no longer in pain and burden
I am not busy even though I live as it is
I live resting and singing
As I no longer exist,
I no longer live for myself
But only live for all

To No Longer Have One's Self, to be The Truth, to be God

To have completely died means
For the self to no longer exist
For one's conceptions to be no more
Is to have completely died
To be rid of one's human body and mind
Is to have completely died
The conceptions and conventions that define us
Are our body and mind
When eliminated,
Only the whole and perfect Truth remains
The Truth cannot disappear; it exists as it is
He who becomes the Truth is the same
He lives for he is the Truth
It is the eternal everlasting world itself
He who has completely died is given oneness
He who is reborn as the universe
Is God of the universe itself
God is the eternal and everlasting energy and light itself

OUR KINGDOM

Our kingdom is the kingdom of one
Our kingdom is the kingdom for all
Our kingdom is the kingdom of the Truth
Our kingdom is the kingdom of life
Our kingdom is the kingdom of resurrection
Our kingdom is the kingdom of heavenly paradise
Ours is the living kingdom

THE TRUTH WANDERER

People live
For their own livelihood and happiness
But only I live in foreign lands miles away
Where everything is of strange waters,
Unfamiliar faces
And communication is difficult
I hope for man to be reborn as the Truth
I teach the Truth
My teaching is that to let go is to have all
There is nowhere in this world for me to be,
Nowhere to dwell
I wander from here to there
Teaching what the Truth is

True Reality

When the false delusions of the mind are no more
Only the Truth remains

On heaven and earth
For those with false delusions,
Death exists
For those with the Truth
Death cannot be found on heaven and earth

The life and death of heaven and earth
Depends on the minds of men

For those without the Truth, heaven and earth are dead
For those with the Truth, heaven and earth lives

By condition man comes and lives
By this condition he goes
But in the world of the Truth
All is one

Those who are born again in the kingdom of heaven while living
Live on as it is even without body
In the perfect kingdom which is one, the Truth
Those who are reborn as a perfect Truth while living
Live in the world of the Truth
Even without body

Man lives as he does now
For the true Soul and Spirit of the universe is what is real

In the perfect world,
There is no mind of attachments
No karmic sins
Man is no sinner
And does not live imprisoned as a sinner
All is one with the Truth
All is the Truth itself
Death does not exist
The individual and the whole are one
Within the individual, the whole
Within the whole, the individual
All creation is one
It is the world of true reality
It is the world of the Truth

CONDITION

The world spins
The world changes
That the world spins
Is due to condition
But it is changing
A million different changes are due to the condition
Condition is the cause in and of itself

ALL IS ONE

Into the clear blue sky I send my heart
When I do not exist
When I become the universe
All in heaven and earth is one
Heaven and earth is of one body
All of its creations know no death
It lives as it is
To be as it is
It is freedom; it is liberation

THE CYCLE OF GOD

For the consciousness of man to be
For the mind of man to be
Changed into God,
The human self,
The whole of it should exist no more
By God's approval
One is reborn as God
For the cycles to coincide
All should be absent but the Truth, God itself
So that one's own cycle coincides
To be reborn as God
For only those who become God
May live in the kingdom of God

Those Who Become God Live
in the Eternal Kingdom of Heaven

Since I have no individual mind
And I become the mind of God,
The whole of the universe, great nature itself, is me
For it is the world of light, the world of the living itself
It is the eternal and everlasting energy and light itself
I have become this itself so I live forever
Great nature is this itself so it lives forever
Here is where the kingdom of heaven is

When the whole dwells in the individual
The individual lives
All creation is living
The reason that man is dead
Is due to the mind of attachment that he holds
When this mind is no more, it is freedom, liberation
When this mind is no more,
It is the eternal life, the kingdom of heaven
The God of the very beginning lives
The God of the very beginning is life
He who has become this God lives

In the individual the whole dwells
So that the individual is God
The individual is the whole
The whole is the individual
The mind of God is not of attached mind

The mind of God exists as it is
It is a mind separate from all
This mind does not change
This mind is eternal and everlasting
He who has this mind is one reborn into heaven
He who has this mind is one
Reborn into the kingdom of heaven
For this world is living, it is the kingdom of light
Light is life
It is light for it is living
Because I lack nothing,
The eternal, imperishable world is in me
And I am the master of this world

The existence and non-existence of this world is one
There is a picture on one side of a coin
And though there is none on the other side
A coin is still a coin
The picture of the material world is the whole of creation
It is the world where such creation lives
It is the world of God
For the world of God is absent of death
And everything is the embodiment of God
Everything lives
This earth and heaven do not exist separately
For when this earth becomes the kingdom of heaven
The kingdom will exist
That is to say
If mankind does not live in the kingdom of heaven
The kingdom is of no use
Now is the time for mankind to live
Everyone comes and goes from this world once
But should it be that

While some live eternally, born in the kingdom of heaven
Others die?
Let us seek penitence
Let us repent
Let us seek absolution of sin
Let us live free of worry or pain
In the eternal everlasting world of light and freedom

When this earth becomes heavenly paradise
We live selflessly for others
We live as one
For we are all
For all is I as one
Live the mind, that is one
For a life according to nature's flow
Is the mind of great nature
All we do is to live according to nature's flow
When man lives selflessly for others
The world will be a better place to live
Though his body may die
The Soul and Spirit of the universe, which is God,
Lives on in the world as it is
It is to live absent of life and death
Eternal and everlasting world of oneness

LIVE AS IT IS

Be as it is
Live as it is
All is living
All is the Truth, oneness
All is alive
All is free of troubles and worries
All lives

Knowing and Becoming the True Mind

Knowing God
Is only for those who have become God
Even knowing the mind
Is something only those with a true mind can do

The mind of man is a mind of delusion
Such delusion is his form
And he lives according to his form
Such delusion is personal sin
The body, which has delusion, is original sin
And cleansing comes through Maum Meditation

He who has cleansed his mind and has true mind
The infinite mind of the universe itself
Knows the true meaning of the mind,
Can see God, and is God
It is to eliminate all false minds
Let only God, the Truth, remain
Be reborn as God
And live in the eternal, everlasting world

FAITH

Faith generally means
To believe in a subject
But true faith
Is to believe in what we have within
To merely believe in a subject
Is to believe in an image of one's own delusions
To have faith in what is within,
When the mind believes, it is true belief
This is true faith
To believe in a vague truth,
Is to believe in a truth
Of one's own conceptions and conventions
Delusion believes in a truth of delusion
To have faith in that the Truth exists in oneself,
Is for those who have the Truth to believe with their hearts
True faith is to believe with the heart

When one's mind is true,
True faith is to believe that the Truth exists
In the Bible
To believe with the heart and answer with the mouth
This means to acknowledge that
The Truth, Jesus Christ, exists in one's heart
And answer with the mouth, "The Truth, Jesus Christ exists"
This means to be enlightened,
To receive an answer to a prayer of penitence

World beyond world is a world of completion
World beyond world is a world alive
World beyond world is a world as it is
World beyond world is a world of it' s own accord
World beyond world is a world of the mind of great nature
World beyond world is a world of oneness
World beyond world is a world, eternal and everlasting
World beyond world is a world of God, Buddha
World beyond world is a world of the next life
That can be known only through death
World beyond world is a world of heavenly paradise

TRANSCENDENCE FROM RELIGION

Transcendence from a religion is not
Another religion beyond a religion
Transcendence itself is transcendence from religion
People frequently ask me,
 'Is Maum Meditation a religion?'
Religion is about following the teachings
Christianity teaches the word of Jesus Christ
Buddhism teaches the word of Buddha
Maum Meditation is cleansing the mind
Finding the Truth within
And being reborn as the Truth

Cleansing the mind is a prayer of repentance
He who has no sin lives, born again as God
As he is God itself and becomes the child of God
This God is the scripture itself; this God is the Truth itself

The word is the Truth itself
It is he who has become the Truth
It is he who has reached the world beyond religion
He who has cleansed his mind and received absolution of sin
Has reached the world beyond religion
As he lives in the world where only those who become God live
This God has no religion
And life itself is the Truth, freedom, and liberation

A world free from religion is a world beyond religion
One becomes the Truth for the self no longer exists
And he who has become the Truth lives a life of the Truth

A Perfect Plan for Living in the World

He whose consciousness is dead
Lives in his own conceptions and conventions
Since he speaks and acts from his own viewpoint,
His mind dwells in his own experiences
One with knowledge of delusions, which is not the Truth,
Pretending as if it is true
What he says and how he acts is from his own viewpoint
He who no longer exists and has become
The highest, widest, and biggest living consciousness of God,
Speaks and acts the Truth
Carries out this plan as the Truth
This is the Truth

A perfect plan without changes
Can be presented
This plan made from the viewpoint of the perfect God
Is eternal and everlasting
Religion, philosophy, ideology, politics, economics,
Academics, society and living,
Which are considered and judged from the great consciousness,
Are all part of a perfect plan
Man can live a life of comfort
Because God is perfect
God can present the perfect plan

THE PERFECT PLAN FOR MANKIND

Man must
Go beyond the whole of
Religion, ideology, philosophy, politics, economics
And living in society
And come up with a perfect plan
The perfect plan is
For all to become one and live as one
And for everyone to live as one
Without the separation between you and I
To be born as the Truth
That is one body and mind of the universe

CREATION OF THE UNIVERSE

When the light of God that is heaven and earth itself
Exists in man, that is also called the mind
The mind of man made into one with the light of God
Is the creation of the light of God
To live caged in the mind filled with one's own attachments
Is the life of a sinner
Who lives life caged in his own prison

After he has sought absolution of all sin, he has no sin
Like being freed from his prison
He who has no sin is free; he is liberated
To live life as it is without life and death
Is to live as it is
One can always live in the normal state of mind
Because one lives life, but does not live in it
And has no mind of the fact that he lives
He lives life simply as it is
Everything he does
He does with the absence of mind and lives as it is
So that he lives a life of true mercy, true love, true compassion
Which is a life according to nature's flow
One who lives life with self
Lives a life of death, not a life according to nature's flow,
Is dead and trapped in hell

MAUM (THE MIND)

He who is trapped within himself
Lives with the mind trapped within himself
Man lives thinking that his body is his master
But the movements and actions of the body
Are done by the mind

He who lives with delusions and demons in his mind
Thinks and acts according to his delusions
Because of human mind,
People's thoughts are of a million different sorts
Although the same event is observed
The mind that arises
Is different for everyone

That mind comes from
The life one has lived according to his own image
That image is his mind
To cleanse the mind
Is to eliminate the delusional mind
Of attachments that constitute who he is

To eliminate all memories of one's lived life,
Which are the attachments formed due to one's environment,
To eliminate the body,
Which lived housing the demon within,

Is to return to the place
Before the existence of one's own thoughts
When that mind, which is the consciousness,
Becomes one with God or Buddha
It is the highest, widest, and biggest
So that the self no longer exists
To have returned to God or Buddha itself
Is the mind that is reborn as the mind of God
The mind of God or Buddha
God is the Truth
God is the eternal, everlasting energy and light itself
He who has returned to that energy and light
And has been reborn as that energy and light lives eternally
To have that energy and light within
To have the infinite universe
That is the biggest, highest, and widest universe itself
Is to be absent of one's own delusional self,
Thus, only the Truth remains within
All this in itself is the eternal heaven

People,
Those of you who have a true mind are the rich in true spirit
Lacking nothing
Those of you who have become
The energy and light, the Truth, in and of itself
Live without curiosity, questions or doubts
With a mind of pure emptiness, severed from all
That mind, which has become God
Does not discern rights or wrongs
Has no conflict since it accepts everything
And lives as it is and exists as it is

From the perspective of a great mind,
To live selflessly
And live for others
That life itself is for oneself;
It is one's own life
To live not within oneself
But live for the whole,
Live for others
This is the perfect plan for mankind
To become one

May mankind realize that all faults are his own
May mankind do Maum Meditation
To cleanse and eliminate himself
So that everyone lives as one

A Mind That Is the Largest, the Highest, and the Widest Is God, Buddha, and Divinity Itself

The mind of man
Lives self-centeredly
Bound to oneself without being aware of it
God is omniscient and omnipotent
Omniscience is the mind of the universe, God
Omnipotence is the body of the universe
The forms of all creation are the form of God,
Which is the universe
The state of God does not seem to exist for man cannot see it
But that non-existence exists
For everything to be brought forth as existence
The principle that one exists because of the other
According to condition
Is through the omnipotent body of the universe
There is no place in the universe where God does not dwell
God exists as light, as it is

Light is life
It is living
It lets live
It is the eternal kingdom of heaven
Since the life of all creation lives as that itself,
It is called light
For those who have this light in their minds,
They don't say "There is no mind."
They say "The mind exists."

To look for the sky above from the bottom of a deep well,
The sky is nowhere to be found
But after we come out of the well we can see the sky, it exists
When we become the biggest, widest and highest God within,
Which exists before the infinite universe
We can see and become the body and mind of the universe
That, in and of itself, is light
We are able to see in brightness
It is the master of creation itself
It is both the mother and father of creation itself
One who is not reborn
Has no way to live eternally
The eternal Truth is
God who created the universe before the universe
There is only God in the universe
And the one God is the Truth
There is none that can live without becoming the Truth
When we become the widest, biggest and highest God itself
We can understand
The true meaning of omniscience and omnipotence
Omniscience is to know the true meaning of the universe
It is to know the fundamentals of the Truth, God
The whole of creation of this world will disappear
But the creator before the universe
Who is the Great Soul and Spirit
Is eternal everlasting energy and light itself
There is none that can live without becoming this itself

To know the fundamentals of the world
Is to rightly see and rightly understand everything
Everything is the Truth just as we see it, just as it is
With delusional thoughts, however,
The Truth cannot be seen

We draw an image of our own delusions
The fundamental principle of the world is simply one
He who knows that everything lives is one who lives
He who lives is the wise one
He is the omniscient one
As that God lives,
The life of God
Is to act the Truth without mind
So that speech and action are one
He who is bound to his own conceptions and conventions
Lives his life in those conceptions and conventions
And acts according to them
Let us widen our minds to act the Truth
Let us all live

The Voice of the Truth

Where we come from
Why we live
And where we go
Through the time that has passed
Many people have come and gone,
However
No one has been able to give us a clear answer
Even if there is an answer,
No one leads us, no one knows the way to go

For man to become perfect
He must become the omniscient and omnipotent God
This is the only way for man to know the answer
God is
The one God which is the infinite universe itself
Which has a body and mind of itself
Unless one is reborn as the consciousness of God
He will never know the answer
Unless the self within him dies
To become the master of the whole
In the kingdom of God, the world of Buddha
He will never know the answer
When we see from the viewpoint of God,
Everything in the universe can be understood
We will know the answer

God is the eternal and everlasting Truth
The Truth is what is living
The Truth is before the Alpha and after the Omega
The Truth is to just be as it is
Because the new heaven and earth is also the world of God
It has been existent as it is
When the consciousness of man
Becomes as high, as wide, and as big as God
He will have the kingdom of God
That is the new heaven and earth
This is because man can now have in him
What he was lacking before
God has made it so that the minds of men can be God
This is so because man is made to resemble God
Man is also the one God of the pure emptiness
The child of God
One with God and God himself
To live is the life of man

Where we come from, why we live
And where we go
Although we just exist, live as it is
And there is no such thing as coming and going
Our existence is ourselves
We must live in order for everything to exist
For the existence of all creation is
Meaningless without man
By the will of man, the whole of creation exists
Because only man knows
The existence and non-existence of creation
And only man understands this
If man did not exist,
The existence of heaven and earth would have no meaning

Man is reborn as the master
Lives everlasting life knowing no death
Lives eternally as one

Becoming complete must be achieved
While we are living on this earth
As the next world is this world, it exists as it is
The fortune of worthy deeds remains the same
In the real world

Heaven Can Only Be Seen and its Will Can Only Be Known by Those Who Have Become Heaven

The clear blue sky
Is so high and so blue
Everything in this world looks this way
One can see only as much as he knows, as much as he sees
Man and heaven and earth is that itself
Man does not know that it is the fundamentals of God

Just as the clouds hide the sky
Heaven cannot be seen because one's self exists
Heaven can be seen by those
Who do not have their individual minds
The life form living in heaven is God, Buddha
It is the heaven before all creation
And true image of heaven before all creation
Is the image of God, Buddha

Even though
There are millions of different forms of clouds in the sky
The sky remains as it is
Likewise, even though
There are millions of different forms in this world
The true nature of heaven is to exist as it is
Because people have their own minds
People cannot see heaven nor can they understand heaven's will
Only those who have become heaven can know heaven's will
They live doing the work of heaven

Heaven is where the world came from
And where it will return
Within heaven,
The perfect world is the place of heavenly bliss
It is the kingdom where only the Truth exists and lives
That kingdom can only be entered while one is alive
That kingdom can only be entered by those
Who have become one with heaven while living
That kingdom can only be entered by those
Who have become heaven itself

Only those written in heaven's Book of Life may live
When he has become the God inside his heart
And has become God of heaven
The God in his heart
Believes that God is in his heart
And answers with his mouth that God lives
Only those with the seal of heaven that he is one with God
May live
Those who no longer have their selves and have died
Are reborn as the children of God
And will live eternally as they are God themselves
Those who have the kingdom of heaven in them
Will live because they have the kingdom of heaven
Only the people whose minds are God, perfection itself,
Can live
And they are reborn into and live in the kingdom of God
Though God is omniscient and omnipotent
It itself is the mind of great nature
And absent of any mind of that
Those who know the will of heaven
All have minds as large as heaven
Such people understand the meaning of the Truth

Because they have heaven in them
Heaven lacks nothing
For it is the highest, the biggest, the widest, and perfect
Heaven is to exist on its own and as it is
To live as it is, that is the will of heaven
It is heaven
With the impure mind of man
With the stained mind of man
Heaven can neither be seen nor heard
He who has become heaven can hear the sounds of heaven
And lives in accordance with heaven's will
He does heaven's deeds
Knows all creation
Knows all creation is alive
Because it is the eternal energy itself
It is to know the everlasting Great Soul and Spirit,
Which is the mind of all creation

Human wisdom does not exist
Because man is not able to have heaven inside him
Thus, there is an absence of wisdom
The wise are those who have the mind and body of heaven
The wise are those who have been reborn as God of heaven
Only God has wisdom
God itself is wisdom
Just as the eternal Truth is
The body and mind of the infinite heaven
He who is reborn as that body and mind
Is God of heaven itself
He is the eternal and unchanging energy itself
Because that itself is the Truth, he lives forever
The original body and mind, which is the original master
Is the Truth itself, and thus, it knows no death

Because he has
The eternal unchanging body and mind of heaven
He will live forever and ever
The whole of creation appears as God
Which is the eternal unchanging energy and light itself
So even though the representation of creation disappear
The representation, which is God, energy and light,
Continues to live on
That is the complete kingdom
The origin of the Truth is the shape of every creation
The shapes live for they are perfect
He who is trapped in his own attachments eventually dies
But he who repents and has become
God, the Truth, the energy and light
Is one who is blessed by heaven

Although The Original World Is Already Enlightened, There Was No One Enlightened Until Now

Enlightenment is achieved
When one's own consciousness is
The same as the already enlightened world
That is enlightenment
Man lives trapped in his own mold
If there were no way to break the mold
Enlightenment would not be possible
The world is originally the perfect God itself
And since the world, which is the whole, is already enlightened
It is the perfection itself
Because man is trapped in his own grave
And imprisoned in his own cage
He does not know the enlightened world
He does not know the enlightened kingdom of heaven
He does not know the enlightened ultimate bliss
He does not know the enlightened world of true reality

The road to the world of true reality
Is to be freed from sin
To go to the world of the Truth
And go to the enlightened kingdom
It is the kingdom of God, the kingdom of Truth
The world of true reality, the kingdom of one
The perfect world has always existed as it is
But that there is no enlightened person
Is because one's own mind could not become the Truth

Which is the highest, lowest, widest, and biggest
Which is perfect and infinite
Because one's mind could not be reborn as the Truth
Once enlightened,
He will realize there was no one enlightened

TRUE FAITH

Faith is one's own conviction
True faith is when one is confident in his heart
One must believe from one's heart
For it to be true faith
To have true faith is to become one

ACCEPTANCE IS THE GREATEST

Acceptance itself is the greatest of all
For one embraces everything, he has no discernment
He embraces everything
In order for everything to be awakened
To be awakened
Does not mean that one gains enlightenment
By discerning rights and wrongs
To be awakened
Means that one gains enlightenment
By discerning rights and wrongs
Without the mind of discernment
This is acceptance with the mind absent of one's self
Because
One embraces the narrow mind of everything within
This is great compassion and great mercy
It is a great mind and great love
It is also wisdom of life and the mind of great nature
A life by nature's flow is a life of acceptance
Because one is perfect, he does not belong to this or that
This or that is one
Because one lives seeing everything just as it is
He teaches without belonging to the teaching
But just does it; this is acceptance

OUR KINGDOM IS

Our kingdom is the kingdom of one
He who has become one lives in our kingdom
Our kingdom is beyond this world
Our kingdom exists beyond this world
He who lives in this kingdom is complete

● Postscript

I wrote this book to help organize the studies of those who have been meditating diligently.

My will is to make people live. A man who dwells on past failures is unable to progress because he has a negative mind. Conversely, only those who do Maum Meditation with a positive mind can achieve the Truth and live.

I have been putting all my efforts into teaching human completion to all mankind. Only those with patience and endurance are able to accomplish completion. As a bitter medicine can produce good results, endurance and persistence give birth to the Truth.

My great hope is for all mankind to truly repent and become perfect.

Appendix
DIALOGUES ON GOD, EXISTENCE AND THE TRUTH

A Special Talk[11]

A DIALOGUE BETWEEN THE GREAT MASTER WOO MYUNG
AND REVEREND JOE GATTIS ON THE TRUTH AND THE UNIVERSE

JOE: Can you explain to me what original sin is?

WOO MYUNG: Original sin has existed since human beings distinguished good from evil. Good and evil exist because people believe so. Indeed, out of all creation only man distinguishes good from evil. Thus, the thought with which we distinguish good from evil is original sin.

JOE: The reason I do Maum Meditation is to gain peace of mind, to get the eternal peace that I am seeking. I am convinced that this is possible through Maum Meditation.

WOO MYUNG: Do you know where God is?

JOE: God is everywhere.

WOO MYUNG: Have you seen God? You are able to see God when your mind is cleansed.

JOE: It is impossible to see God as an image.

WOO MYUNG: I can see God clearly. Everyone here around you can also see God as well.

JOE: I know that practicing Maum Meditation is to wake up from a dream. I am still asleep. I haven't awakened from the dream yet.

---

11 This special talk between the great master Woo Myung and Reverend Joe Gattis took place when Easter was around the corner in 2003. It was to find out the true meaning of the universe, Truth, death and resurrection. At that time Joe Gattis had been a devoted reverend for 27 years. He began Maum Meditation at the time of his visit with Woo Myung in Atlanta, Georgia, U.S.A. The dialogue was also carried in the monthly magazine Maum Sooryun April, 2003.

WOO MYUNG: Human completion cannot be accomplished unless you become God.

JOE: Where did the Truth come from?

WOO MYUNG: The Truth has always existed as it is. It existed before Alpha and will also exist after Omega. The Truth itself is God. Both the Big Bang and Expansion Theories are incorrect. The universe did not become bigger due to explosions.

JOE: I think God existed before the Big Bang and God created the universe. I think the Big Bang is the way God created the universe.

WOO MYUNG: God, the infinite universe, has always existed. It did not form or become bigger by the Big Bang.

JOE: From my childhood, I have tried many ways to reach the Truth. For example, I tried Christianity. The reason this Maum Meditation method is obviously good is that one can very effectively reach the Truth within a very short period of time. Can I think that the Truth, heaven, and the emptiness are one?

WOO MYUNG: They are all the same as it is.

JOE: I thought we would live in the kingdom of heaven after we died, but now I realize how to live in the kingdom when you said that this land becomes heaven when we die while living. Do we continue to live here even though this body dies?

WOO MYUNG: Your soul is what keeps on living. You can welcome Jesus only if your mind becomes the mind of Jesus. Only when your mind becomes one with that of Jesus are you able to become Jesus. There is only one sin in this world. It is the sin of disbelieving in and not becoming Jesus. Jesus is believed to have accomplished completion by being one with God through dying on the cross. Human completion can only be accomplished when man dies while living. Jesus was completed because he died for the Truth. Now is the time when everybody is able to be born again and to live as God.

JOE: It is also written in the Bible that all sins except one can be forgiven. The only sin that cannot be forgiven is disbelieving in God. When a disciple asked Jesus in the Bible whether a heathen who was doing what Jesus did was against us or for us, Jesus answered that he was not against us as long as he was teaching the same thing that Jesus taught.

WOO MYUNG: Now is the time for everyone to become Jesus. There are two problems in modern Christianity. First, Christians believe in the Jesus who died two thousand years ago instead of believing in the true Jesus. Second, they do not truly repent their sins. They cannot hear the voice of God until they are confessed of their sins. True repentance means absolution. Those who believe in the true Jesus are born again in the kingdom of heaven while living and eternally live a heavenly life there. Jesus and Shakyamuni[12] only spoke of the true Jesus or Buddha, but now is the time for everyone to become the true Jesus or Buddha.

JOE: What is the Messiah?

WOO MYUNG: The Savior is one who absolves us of our sins. Because it cleanses our minds, Maum Meditation is a study of absolving sin.

JOE: Has the Jesus of two thousand years ago come again?

---

12 We commonly refer to Buddha as the historical founder of Buddhism, but his real name is Siddhartha Gautama. However, he is widely known as 'Shakyamuni,' which means 'sage of the Shaky clan.'

Woo Myung: No, Jesus does not come again but has always just been here from the earliest times. We have only masked Jesus with our minds because we have not been able to absolve our sins. When we absolve our sins through cleansing our minds, we become one with Jesus, and that is salvation. When we wipe out our sins from our minds, God gives answers to all our questions within us. We have to believe in God within us and confess our sins. Then, the world in which all creation becomes one is supposed to be accomplished. After all, we cannot be born in the kingdom of heaven unless we become Jesus himself.

Joe: Do you believe in Jesus?

Woo Myung: Which Jesus are you talking about?

Joe: The Jesus who died on the cross.

Woo Myung: I do. However, I believe in the Jesus who has existed before Abraham. But the problems are: First, people believe in the Jesus who died two thousand years ago. They do not believe in the true Jesus. Second, people do not truly repent their sins to God. If they only do this wholeheartedly, the whole world can become one. Does this answer your question?

Joe: Yes.

Woo Myung: It needs to be emphasized that people should believe in the true Jesus. The shape of Jesus whom we know from history is not the Truth, but the true Jesus is.

Joe: Was Jesus the Son of God?

Woo Myung: Sure. One who dedicates all to God is the Son of God. When you pray in church, don't you also call God 'Heavenly Father'? You are also the Son of God.

Joe: What is God who you believe in?

Woo Myung: God is within me and is the whole universe as it is. There is not a single thing that is not God, and all things in creation are the Son of God as well as God himself. God is the infinite universe which existed before the infinite universe. The sun, stars, the earth, and all creation did not originate from a physical existence but from the infinite universe.

JOE: What is the Truth?

WOO MYUNG: The infinite universe is the Truth. The Truth was originally named God, Buddha, or Allah, and so forth. All these names mean the same Truth. The true mind, true nature, is the Truth.

JOE: If the universe is emptiness, then the Truth is also emptiness, isn't it?

WOO MYUNG: Is the infinite universe something that actually exists or not?

JOE: It exists.

WOO MYUNG: That existence in itself is everything. The original universe - the place of God - has nothing, but does it not have the body and mind of man? In Christianity, the body is called the Holy Spirit and the mind, God, is called the Holy Father. If you were to study this Meditation and find your true body and mind, it itself is you. When you throw away your own body and mind, you can find your true body and mind. It is possible to become like that when your body and mind become the infinite universe.

JOE: How can I reach the universe?

WOO MYUNG: When you seek absolution of sin, you can reach the universe. When you cleanse your original and personal sins completely, you become the universe.

JOE: How can I really confess my sins and repent?

WOO MYUNG: Real confession and true repentance is to offer yourself to the infinite universe completely. What you call 'yourself' consists only of your body and mind.

When you throw away both of these, you become the infinite universe.

JOE: Does resurrection really happen?

WOO MYUNG: Consider this: when everything in the universe disappears, what is left?

JOE: There is nothing left.

WOO MYUNG: The infinite universe, itself, exists. If this notebook were to totally burn and disappear, what would remain? If you were to disappear, what would remain? Does the infinite universe still remain or not?

JOE: Yes, it still remains.

WOO MYUNG: Then, who is it?

JOE: It is 'me'.

WOO MYUNG: Does the infinite universe die or not?

JOE: No, it does not die.

WOO MYUNG: Indeed, it is 'you'; that is what it means to be born again. Although the human body dies, the true body and mind remain as the infinite universe. That is to be born again. Do you believe in the infinite universe?

JOE: I now know that I am the infinite universe. I have never heard this kind of thinking anywhere. Does karma really exist?

WOO MYUNG: 'Sin' is karma.

JOE: Karma is man's thought, isn't it?

WOO MYUNG: Yes, that is so. The reason why everybody has his or her own thoughts and ideas is that everyone has different karma.

JOE: Is God 'love'?

WOO MYUNG: God is the greatest love. The greatest love is to become one.

JOE: Everyone thinks that we cannot become the children of God without true love.

WOO MYUNG: The mind of man does not have true love.

Frankly speaking, even the act of helping others is done with one's own mind of doing a good deed. Only God can truly love.

JOE: Are love, the Truth, and the universe all the same?

WOO MYUNG: Yes.

JOE: When the body dies, what happens?

WOO MYUNG: Those who have the body and mind of the universe live eternally in heaven while those who don't cannot become free from their individual conceptions.

JOE: I know that I am living tied to my 'self'. After I do Maum Meditation I would like to live in heaven. After I die, what will happen to the memories of my life?

WOO MYUNG: After death, you know nothing, but if you were to try you could know everything. Just as you have thrown away your memories, the memories still exist, don't they? You just eliminate whatever conceptions are attached to those memories.

JOE: If I see God, what happens to me?

WOO MYUNG: When you see God, 'you' will die, just as it is written in the Bible. The 'self' who was once bound to your past conceptions dies and you are born again as God.

JOE: If we came from the universe and we return to the universe, why does the present life exist? The universe is heaven, and if I am the existence from heaven, why did I leave heaven and come to this world?

WOO MYUNG: That would have no meaning just as staying forever in the emptiness would. The significance of this Maum Meditation is to be born again with the true body and mind of the universe and live eternally to save the others that are existent. To save all creation in existence is the ultimate goal of this study. From the viewpoint of the universe, everything in it is the Son of God and God itself. Everything in creation has been complete in the kingdom of God as it is. However, the consciousness of human beings is dead due to their original and personal sins. When such sins have been absolved, man is born in heaven, and every creation is saved by the will of God. The universe is originally 'emptiness'; it exists on its own and exists as it is. Because man exists, 'I' exist just as trees and flowers exist.

JOE: I think that our birth has meaning.

WOO MYUNG: Indeed, birth has meaning in itself and so does practicing this Maum Meditation.

JOE: I know. Where is the universe?

WOO MYUNG: It just exists here as it is. It exists on its own.

JOE: If this real world is merely a dream, where is the true reality?

WOO MYUNG: It exists in heaven. Then, where is heaven?

JOE: Here.

WOO MYUNG: That's right. You will know heaven when you come to it.

JOE: Do we have the memories after we throw away our memories?

WOO MYUNG: Yes.

JOE: Though we finish the meditation, do we have emotions? Or are there emotions?

WOO MYUNG: Emotions exist but one no longer dwells in such emotions. Although one is happy, he does not dwell in his happiness. There is no longer such thing as delusional thought and he lives on as God.

Q&A's on Mind, the Truth, and Maum Meditation[13]

Does Good And Evil Originally Exist?

Both good and evil exist in the conceptions of man, but do not originally exist. That this is good or this is bad only exists according to one's own conceptions. When seen from God's viewpoint, good and evil do not exist. God is the great love. Even without such rules and laws, the great love lives for others without hate, but with love; it lives selflessly in true goodness.

When one does good deeds being aware of doing them for others, it is not true goodness but the delusional thoughts (demons) doing good deeds for its own interest. If it had been said that murder were not a sin, then it would not be a sin. A lion kills its prey everyday but, because it does not know whether it is good or evil, good and evil does not exist for the lion. Man must be free of both good and evil for him to no longer have good and evil.

Good and evil exist in the minds or conceptions of men. Both good and evil exist only in one's own mind, which has been taught good and evil. He who has become God lives life for others and is free from good and evil.

---

13 These are the answers the great teacher Woo Myung gave in response to questions about the Truth from leaders of the religious world and from esteemed scholars.

What Is Original Sin?

Original sin has existed ever since our ancestors distinguished what is good and what is evil, ever since they picked good and ate it, and ever since they picked evil and ate it. Our ancestors 'picked and ate' both good and evil because they put good and evil in them. Because we are born of those ancestors we carry this original sin. The shape of my ancestors who put good and evil in them, was passed on to me and is my shape. I was born carrying the original sin.

Where are Heaven and Hell?
How is one Able to See Heaven?
What Does it Mean to Live in Heaven
and How Is that Life?

Both heaven and hell exist inside oneself. Both heaven and hell are the universe. One who becomes the original God of the universe is the God of the universe as it is, and he has the kingdom of God, the universe, within him. That is to live in heaven. The kingdom of heaven where there is no past, present, or future is where everything is living. One can go there only while living.

Hell is the life that those who are bound to their own conceptions and habits live according to those conceptions and habits. Just as they suffer from their delusion while living in this world, they will have the same suffering in hell after dying because they live with their dead consciousness bound to the yoke of their conceptions and habits.

He whose consciousness is the mind of the infinite universe, God, can see the kingdom of heaven. He who is born again with this consciousness lives in heaven even while living because he is complete God.

Life in heaven is great freedom and great liberation. Although there is no such thing as joy, the life is full of utmost joy. It can never be boring because the millions of years that pass are just a day, unrestrained and free.

Does Karma Really Exist?

Karma is original sin along with one's own personal sin. This karma is something that every human being has.

Where Do We Go After We Die?

Those who have delusions live with the illusion of those delusions after death. But those who have become the Truth live in the kingdom of heaven eternally.

What Happens After The Human Body Dies?

When a person's body dies, if his consciousness has been awakened, he will live. But if his consciousness was not born again as God, he will die.

Are We Able to Remember and See Our Own Lives after We Die?

Those who die still holding on to their attachments cannot remember their lives because their consciousness is dead. However, others who are born again as the Truth have a living consciousness and can remember and see everything even after they die since both life and death are the same.

How Can We Truly Repent Our Sins?

To make penitence is to repent of our sins. Man thinks that nothing is ever his fault or that he has done nothing wrong, but this concept is wrong. Man lives with his attachments of wants and desires so everything he does is centered on himself. Thus, he lives his life farther and farther from God or Buddha. When a person reflects on himself, discards his self-centered life, and continuously eliminates his self, he will come to realize he himself is the real demon.

Since our existence consists only of our body and mind, we can truly repent our sins by eliminating our body and mind, thus eliminating our existence all together. God appears to the extent that we repent our sins, and to the extent he appears we are able to hear the replies to our prayers. We have to keep on dying until the God within us acknowledges that we have died completely and that we are born into the kingdom of heaven. He who is not complete is curious to know only about his own attachments.

Why Must We Eliminate Ourselves On Our Own?

We must cleanse the sins we have committed on our own. It is the God within who kills our delusional self. When God expels and conquers our demons, we are born again as the children of God. I, not as an individual self but as a child of God, must expel my demon self. And I must win the victory within myself. To win that victory, I must kill it on my own.

Why Must We Throw Away the Good Deeds That We Have Performed?

The good deeds we performed, we did with our own minds. When our good deeds remain in our minds they are not true goodness at all. The only thing that is true is the universe and the Truth which is just as it is and as we see it. The only goodness is the God of the universe and none other. In order to find goodness, we must throw away the delusion that we have done good deeds, for it is only a delusion.

If We Must Throw Away Everything, Must We Also Throw Away Our Religious Faith That We Have Held Up To This Point?

The religious faith that humans have is not based on the true meaning of what the religion teaches. But rather, people recklessly give themselves up to their religion without knowing the true meaning of its words. The teachings of religion are no different than emptying the mind. Thus, we must throw away idolized belief that is based on wants and attachments. We must throw away the false meaning of faith so as to know that God is truly inside us. This is why we must throw away human faith. When we throw away our human faith, true faith remains. When we throw away our human faith, we are able to see God. When we throw away our human faith we can become God.

We can only acknowledge that the perfect, original God is within when we throw away all idolized things of delusion.

IT IS SAID IN THE BOOK OF REVELATIONS THAT ALL FAITH SHALL BE DISCARDED AT THE SECOND ADVENT OF JESUS CHRIST. WHAT DOES THAT MEAN?

Discarding faith means believing in God, the Truth, by eliminating idolizing faith. We are able to acknowledge the true God when we are born again as the children of God. There are millions of denominations of religions even though there exists only one Truth. This is because human faith of today is not on the right path.

Everything that the saints have said is the Truth. When we truly repent and truly seek absolution of sin, we will have true faith and become one. Truth has been carried forth through the religious faith up until now which was sufficient in the past. But now, through cleansing our minds, we have found one way to the Truth.

The New Testament contains the prophecy of a new promise, and when this prophecy is fulfilled all will become one, all will be complete, and the kingdom of heaven will be built. Only those absolved of sin can know the true meaning of this prophecy. People do not know the true meaning of the prophecy because they do not repent their sins and hope for the prophecy to be fulfilled according to their own delusional thoughts.

WILL EVERYONE BE UNCONDITIONALLY SAVED AT THE SECOND ADVENT OF JESUS CHRIST AS THE BIBLE PROPHESIED?

Salvation means to be born in the kingdom of Truth. Even though the kingdom is originally complete, people are dead because of their sins that confine them. Those who free themselves from the chains of sins shall be saved. Only those who are free from the chains of sins and are sealed with the Truth shall be saved.

Only those who are recorded in the Book of Life shall be saved. Only those who confess with their mouths that the Truth is within shall be saved. They will be judged with sheep and goats and the sinful will die, buried in their sins.

Is Salvation a Reality?

For those who are not saved while living there will be no salvation. Salvation means that we are born again as the children of God, the Truth, through the death of one's self. Those who are the Truth will live in the kingdom of heaven because they are the Truth. Unless we are born as the children of God while living, we shall die when this body dies.

Anyone who repents his sins, cleanses his mind, is absolved and can enter the kingdom of heaven. Only the children of God who are God itself can go to the kingdom of heaven. If we seek penitence now and are absolved of sin we will enter into heaven. Thus, salvation is a reality.

What Does it Mean that God Is Both Love and Judgment?

God loves, raises, feeds, and gives life to all things in creation. Because man commits sins and is unable to be free from them, he is said to be judged. God tries to save all this with love but because man does not believe in the God of Truth inside him, he is judged.

What Does it Mean that God Is Love?

God is love. We live according to the will of God because God is omniscient and omnipotent; God is love as it is. However, man does not appreciate this. Once we become one with God, we are able to acknowledge that God is love itself because all creation lives by the virtue of God.

Do Love, Truth, and the Universe Mean the Same Thing?

True love is the love that God, or the Truth, gives without the mind of having done it. This is the same as the universe which existed before the universe.

What Happens When We See God?

When we see God, our individual self dies, and we become God. Hence, we have the wisdom to know the God of life. Just as knowing God is the essence of wisdom, when we are rid of all delusions, the wisdom of true righteousness comes forth, and we are born in the eternal kingdom because we have the wisdom.

Can Man Be God?

God has always existed. God is the Truth itself. Man cannot become the original God, but he can be born again as a child of God. Only God can give birth to us as the Truth. We are born again with our bodies that we received from the original God and thus, we are the children of God. Even though we are born again from the original God, we are one with God. Christianity says that man cannot become God, which means that the original God has always existed and is the creator who created everything in completion, and we are creations of the original God, born again in the kingdom of God. We are born again as God because we have completely died.

Where Is the Universe?

The universe exists as it is. This universe becomes the world where everything becomes one and man is born again as the Truth when it is in him. The universe is within all the material things, and all those things are one. Therefore, those who have the universe outside of them are full of delusions, but those who have the universe within them live.

What Is the Truth?

The Truth is the true state before the universe that we know. The Truth is the one God that exists within the total emptiness. It is the body and the mind of the Truth. Those who are born again as the body and mind of the Truth are the children of God. It is this true state, which created the universe; it is this true state, which is the kingdom of heaven. The Truth is the eternally unchangeable, which exists everywhere in the universe, and is the universe as it is. In the viewpoint of the Truth, all creation is born in the kingdom of completion.

How Do We Reach the Truth?

The Truth is the universe within oneself. Those who have discarded their sins can reach the Truth. A person consists of body and mind, and those who have eliminated their body and mind and have thrown them away, can reach the Truth.

Why Have Our Memories Been Stored Instead of Being Eliminated?

Due to original sin, all of us have different minds of want and desire. Such minds are our memories, our attachments. Those attachments remain in our mind. We have those memories in the mind.

Can We Still Remember Everything Even though We Eliminate our Memories?

When we eliminate the thoughts stored in our memories, images disappear, but we are still able to remember. Whatever we remember comes to our mind when needed.

After We Eliminate Our Memories, Are We Still Able to Feel Emotions? Can We Feel Happy or Sad?

Though we eliminate our memories, we are still able to feel happy or sad. However, what we feel is not due to our cluster of memories, but such emotions created by the true mind with the viewpoint of the universe. Our emotions exist; but actually do not. Our happiness and sorrow do not exist but actually do. It is the Truth that shows these emotions, and thus we are not bound to them.

CAN ILLNESS BE CURED THROUGH CLEANSING OUR MIND? IF SO, HOW?

Illness results from our mind. Since our body and mind are one, how we look and how we behave are based on our mind. Therefore, when we eliminate our mind, we return to the state of completion in which we do not have illness. Thus, illness is cured.

CAN WE SEE THE TRUE MIND WITHOUT EMPLOYING THE METHODS OF MAUM MEDITATION? IS IT IMPOSSIBLE? IF SO, WHY?

Some people who have a lot of endurance and can quiet their minds are able to reach the state of no mind. Such incidents, however, are very rare and last only for a fleeting moment. This is because they are not able to actually empty their minds. Likewise, for those who pray, when they are absent of mind for a split second, think that they have received the Holy Spirit inside them. This too lasts only for a second but does not last permanently.

In Maum Meditation, we cleanse and eliminate our mind. We also eliminate our habits and with this absence of mind and habits, the Truth exists inside us. We die and become complete. Only through the method of eliminating one's body and mind will the original mind appear. When we do not have our individual consciousness and body, we will have the Truth, the universe or the original mind, inside us. The kingdom of heaven is also within man. The original universe dwells within a mind that has the infinite universe.

CAN PEOPLE PRACTICE THIS METHOD IN OTHER PLACES?

We can only find the Truth where the Truth exists. If we try to find the Truth where the Truth does not exist, it is impossible. Even with the right method we have here, it takes efforts to reach the Truth. If a person were to try to achieve the Truth in a place there is no Truth, he would never become the complete Truth no matter how hard he tried. He will remain in the same place till death.

CAN ANY OTHER PERSON TEACH THE TRUTH?

One who is born as the Truth, the complete God, can teach the Truth. Without a true teacher, one cannot reach the Truth through only knowing the method itself due to his lack of understanding and patience.

IS MAUM MEDITATION A RELIGION?

Religion is defined as the belief in and following the words of the Truth. However, people regard religion as the belief in idolized objects without following the words.

Maum Meditation involves cleansing our mind through absolution. In general, people do not know that they are sinners because they do not know what they are doing is wrong. Maum Meditation is not a religion because it lets us eliminate our minds of our own faults as well as our sinful bodies. Those who have become the Truth become religion itself. Ultimately they become the infinite living God itself by eliminating themselves. Those who completely die become God, and they can see God, the Truth, clearly; thus, they themselves are the Truth.

Those who have reached this state acknowledge God and are God as it is. They become religion itself, and they will completely understand the true meaning of religion.

When People Cleanse Their Minds, Will Conventional Religions and Social Systems Be Changed?

When we cleanse our mind, we become the complete Truth itself and truly understand religion and acknowledge the Truth. Also, we live our lives according to nature's flow. We live selflessly for others instead of for ourselves. We make no discernment between others and ourselves, nor is there any discernment between other countries and one's own. We all become one and live without stress, worry, thieves, robbers, and so forth. Therefore, we live for others, and our life is full of comfort and endless bliss.

INTRODUCTION TO THE EIGHT LEVELS
OF MAUM MEDITATION

ENLIGHTENMENT AND THE REPLY TO PRAYER EXIST
ONLY ON THE WAY TO GOD, THE COMPLETE TRUTH

Enlightenment exists when we become the consciousness of God, the complete whole, after expanding individual consciousness.

This is also the reply to prayer. When expanding individual consciousness to that of the consciousness of the universe, we receive the reply to our prayers. That is when we become the completion of the Truth, which is the consciousness of the universe and that consciousness is infinitely high and infinitely wide. When we become God, the complete Truth, we will receive the reply. Thus enlightenment and reply to prayer is the same.

The Eight Levels of Maum Meditation

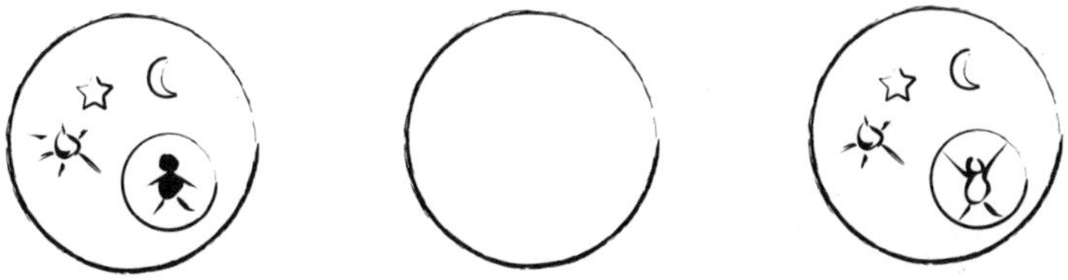

World of Illusion **Original Universe** **World of the Truth**

Level 1	Mind		Knowing I'm the Universe
Level 2			Knowing I Don't Have Mind
Level 3	Body		Knowing the Universe is Within Me
Level 4			Knowing the Body and Mind of the Universe
Level 5	Seeing and Knowing	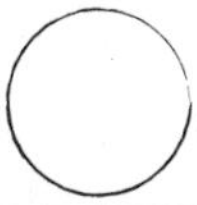	Seeing and Knowing the Body and Mind of the Infinite Universe
Level 6			Seeing and Knowing the Kingdom of Heaven
Level 7	Becoming and Being Reborn		Becoming the Body and Mind of the Universe
Level 8			Being Reborn as the Body and Mind of the Universe in the Perfect Kingdom of Heaven, Receiving the Seal from God on the Forehead and Throughout the Whole Body, and Getting Enlightenment to be Complete

THE LOCATIONS OF MAUM MEDITATION CENTERS

82 Maum Meditation Centers are operating and practicing worldwide, including 50 in Korea.

The Headquarters
Nonsan Main Center
Tel. 82-41-733-8254
Fax. 82-41-733-8707
407-14, Sangwol-myon, Nonsan-city, Chungnam, 320-931, Korea

Argentina
Buenos Aires
TEL. 54-11-4633-6598
FAX. 54-11-4633-6598
Av. Carabobo 1663 Codigo Postal 1406
Cap. Fed Buenos Aires, Argentina

Australia
Sydney
TEL. 61-2-9763-5340
FAX. 61-2-9763-5340
36 Oxford Rd. Strathfield NSW 2135, Australia

Brasil
Sao Paulo
TEL. 55-11-3326-0656
FAX. 55-11-3326-0656
Rua, Afonso Pena, 380, Apt 41
Bom-Retiro, Sao Paulo, Brasil

Canada
Vancouver
TEL. 1-604-516-0709
FAX. 1-604-516-0719
7363 Elwell St. Burnaby B.C. V5E 1L1, Canada

Toronto
TEL. 1-416-730-1949
FAX. 1-416-730-8937
24 Nipigon Ave. Toronto, Ontario, m2m2v8, Canada

Chile
Santiago
TEL. 56-2-732-1981
FAX. 56-2-732-1981
Hanga Roa 739, Recoleta, Santiago, Chile

England
London
TEL. 44-208-412-0134
14 Spinney Close, New Malden, Surrey
KT3 5BQ, England

France
Paris
TEL. 33-1-47-66-29-97
FAX. 33-1-47-66-29-97
20, Rue Leon Jost 75017, Paris, France

Germany
Frankfurt
TEL. 49-61-96-84-533
FAX. 49-61-96-84-533
Friedrich-Ebert Str. 30 65824 Schwalbach, Germany

Hong Kong
Hong Kong
TEL. 852-2572-0107
FAX. 852-2572-0107
Flat A-7 24/F block A Elizabeth House
250-254 Gloucester Road, Hong Kong

Indonesia
Jakarta
TEL. 62-21-725-6888
FAX. 62-21-725-1088
JL. Cibeber I NO 7, Kebayoran Baru, Jakarta, Selatan-Indonesia

Japan
Tokyo
TEL. 81-3-5783-7521
FAX. 81-3-5783-7522
403 Tennoz Duplex 2-11-18 Konan
Minatoku, Tokyodo, Tokyo, Japan

Osaka
TEL. 81-6-6776-5600
FAX. 81-6-6776-5601
6-18 Tojocho, Tennojiku, Osaka, Japan

Saitamaken
TEL. 81-48-258-6901
FAX. 81-48-258-6921
Namiki 4-1-1-1004, Kawaguchishi, Saitamaken, Japan

New Zealand
Auckland
TEL. 64-9-476-2101
FAX. 64-9-476-2101
870 East Coast Rd. Browns Bay,
Auckland, New Zealand

Philippines
Manila
TEL. 63-2-853-5870
FAX. 63-2-853-5870
#5 San Calros St. Magallanes Village,
Makati City, Metro Manila, Philippines

Singapore
Singapore
TEL. 65-6222-4171
FAX. 65-6222-4179
3rd Floor 41 Duxton Hill Road, Singapore

U. S. A.
Atlanta
TEL. 1-678-698-8307
FAX. 1-770-448-7810
6083 Oakbrook Parkway, Norcross,
GA 30093, U. S. A.

Boston
TEL. 1-617-935-1824
FAX. 1-617-923-4014
68 Laurel St, Watertown, MA 02472,
U. S. A.

Chicago
TEL. 1-847-663-9776
FAX. 1-847-663-9760
8101 N Central Ave. Morton Grove,
IL 60053, U. S. A.

Dallas
TEL. 1-469-522-1229
FAX. 1-469-522-1229
3920 Clear Cove Dallas TX 75244, U. S. A.

Guam
TEL. 1-671-646-7222
FAX. 1-671-646-7222
Unit B-1 Benson Villa Apt
184 Tun Jose Camacho St.
7893 Tamuning, Guam, U. S. A.

Hawaii
TEL. 1-808-739-9445
FAX. 1-808-533-2872
1542-c Keeaumoku St. Ho HI 96822, U. S. A.

Houston
TEL. 1-832-541-3523
FAX. 1-713-690-7512
10221 Centre Park Dr. #811 Houston,
TX 77043, U. S. A.

Los Angeles
TEL. 1-213-484-9888
FAX. 1-213-484-2888
226 S. Union Ave. LA, CA 90026,
U. S. A.

New Jersey
TEL. 1-201-461-9890
FAX. 1-201-461-9890
380 Grand Ave. Leonia, NJ 07605,
U. S. A.

New York
TEL. 1-718-353-6678
FAX. 1-718-353-6663
32-02 150th Place, Flushing, NY 11354,
U. S. A.

Orange County
TEL. 1-714-890-0325
FAX. 1-714-890-0365
12235 Beach Blvd. #10 A, Stanton,
CA 90680, U. S. A.

Philadelphia
TEL. 1-215-722-2130
FAX. 1-215-722-2130
1523 Longshore Ave. Philadelphia,
PA 19149, U. S. A.

San Jose
TEL. 1-408-615-0435
FAX. 1-408-615-0155
3216 Humbolt Ave. Santa Clara,
CA 95051, U. S. A.

Seattle
TEL. 1-253-520-2080
FAX. 1-253-520-1299
3410 S 272nd St. Kent , WA 98032,
U. S. A.

Washington
TEL. 1-703-354-8071
FAX. 1-703-354-8071
4076 Championship Dr. Annandale,
VA 22003, U. S. A.